TRANSLATIONS FROM GREEK AND ROMAN AUTHORS

Pliny

D1466493

Pliny
A selection of his letters

TRANSLATED BY CLARENCE GREIG
Lecturer in Education, University of Birmingham

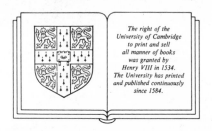

The right of the
University of Cambridge
to print and sell
all manner of books
was granted by
Henry VIII in 1534.
The University has printed
and published continuously
since 1584.

CAMBRIDGE UNIVERSITY PRESS

CAMBRIDGE

NEW YORK   PORT CHESTER   MELBOURNE   SYDNEY

Published by the Press Syndicate of the University of Cambridge
The Pitt Building, Trumpington Street, Cambridge CB2 1RP
40 West 20th Street, New York, NY 10011-4211, USA
10 Stamford Road, Oakleigh, Melbourne 3166, Australia

First published 1978
Reprinted 1991

Printed in Great Britain at the
University Press, Cambridge

Library of Congress Cataloguing in Publication Data

Plinius Caecilius Secundus, C.
Pliny.
(Translations from Greek and Roman authors)
Includes index.
1. Plinius Caecilius Secundus, C. Correspondence.
I. Greig, Clarence, 1935–
II. Title. III. Series.
PA6639.E5G7 1978   876'01   77-91088
ISBN 0 521 21978 7

Contents

Maps and figure

Cover photograph   A detail from Trajan's column showing
    Trajan with a young legate. Reproduced by permission of
    the German Archaeological Institute, Rome.

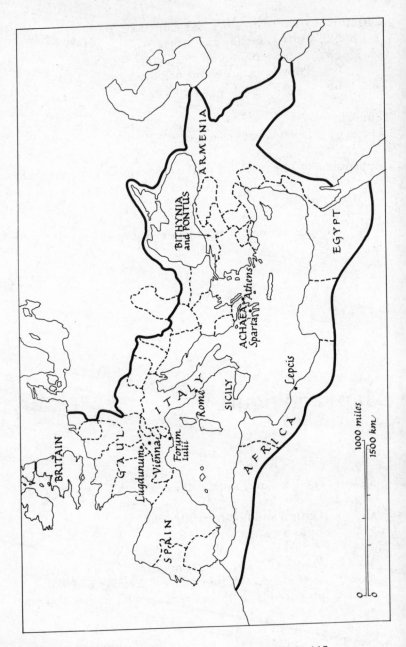

Map 1. The Roman empire at the death of Trajan, A.D. 117

Map 2. Central and northern Italy

Introduction

Pliny

Pliny was born in A.D. 61 at Comum, a small town in the north of Italy. He spent most of his adult life in politics and was for years a member of the **Senate** at Rome. He was also a well-known writer and lawyer. In his will he paid for a set of public baths for the town of Comum. On the side of these baths there was an inscription which tells us this about him.

Pliny's full Roman name was Gaius Plinius Caecilius Secundus. He began his career in Rome by being a junior magistrate, one of the *Board of Ten*. As a member of the Board of Ten, he would act as one of the presidents for a court that dealt with wills and inheritances. He then went out to Syria to be a **military tribune** with the third Gallic legion. Here, although he was an officer in the army, he was busy on administration. He saw no active service. When he returned to Rome, he became a **quaestor** to the Emperor. There were twenty quaestors but only two served the Emperor. The other eighteen quaestors were very often sent abroad to help the governors of the provinces collect the taxes. A good example of one of these is Julius Avitus, in letter 65. The two Quaestors to the Emperor stayed in Rome. They had to read out the Emperor's dispatches in the Senate. So this was a special honour. Then he became **tribune of the people** and soon after a **praetor**. Pliny was not expected to do much in either of these posts. They were more honorary than anything else but they were an important gateway to the highest offices of state. Pliny then became *Head of the Military Treasury* and later *Head of the State Treasury*. In A.D. 100 at the age of 39 he became **Consul**, which was the highest public office in Rome. There were only two Consuls and they took it in turn to preside over the Senate. In Trajan's time the Consuls very often only served for two months of the year. So twenty-four Romans could be Consul in any one year. After that he was appointed *President of the Board that looked after the River Tiber*. Finally in about A.D. 110 he was sent by the Emperor Trajan as his governor, **Legatus Augusti**, to the province of Pontus and Bithynia, which is now modern Turkey.

The names and titles and the exact nature of the offices which Pliny held are not of any great interest in themselves. What matters is we can see from them that of the millions of people that lived in the Roman empire of Pliny's day, he was among the most distinguished. He was very near the top of the pyramid of power. By the end of his life he certainly had done well for himself. He had started off the son of a wealthy man in a small town in northern Italy, far away from the capital city of Rome. He could have stopped where he was and remained a wealthy local landowner. Instead he became the first member of his family to become a **Senator**. The people of Comum would look upon him as a great success. But it was an ambitious and courageous thing to choose a political career in Rome. Pliny was successful and the basis of his success was his work in the Senate. Although he was never a great Roman general or a member of the inner cabinet, he was one of the 600 or so men who helped rule the Roman world.

The Senate was not an easy or safe place to work in. By the time Pliny was a Senator, it was controlled by the Emperor. It was he who now ran the empire. To do this he had his own advisers, friends and civil service but he also used the Senate. In Pliny's lifetime there had been 9 Emperors. Two were forced to commit suicide, 3 were killed and only 4 died naturally. All 9 had been Senators. The Emperor was both a member of the Senate (often he was one of the Consuls) and outside it. We can see the sort of contact which the Emperor and Senators had with each other in the Senate from this letter of Pliny.

How to thank the Emperor

To Severus
You are going to be made Consul. You want me to advise you

on what to say when you thank the Emperor for that honour. There are very many things you could say but it is not easy to choose between them. He is such a good Emperor that you will have plenty to say. I will write and let you know anyway but I would rather tell you face to face.

I have some doubts about this and I do not really know what you should do. When I was going to be made Consul, I did not flatter the Emperor. I also did not act in such a way that others thought I was flattering him. Because I knew what our Emperor was like, I wanted to show myself independent. The highest praise I could give him was to say nothing because I had been made to. I remember how many speeches had been made in honour of the worst Emperor. I felt the best way to honour our Emperor was to make a different sort of speech. And I did not hide from him what I was going to do. I wanted to show him that I meant to make an independent speech. I wanted to show him too that I just had not forgotten to flatter him.

That is what I did. But not everyone likes to do the same. Times change. What we do or do not do, depends as much on things and times as upon ourselves. The Emperor has done some splendid things. This gives you a chance of saying something new, something important, something true. You have many reasons for not doing now what I did then. I do not doubt that. But one thing I am sure of, I had to let you know what I did.

(VI.27)

The nearer you got to the Emperor, the better you did in Roman political life. But the more danger you could be in. The Emperors were always hardest on those who were nearest to them. We have a number of accounts written at the time when Pliny was alive, which tell us what some of the Emperors were like. Many were cruel, suspicious, quick to act, jealous, easily persuaded by others, superstitious, and distrustful, even of members of their own families. Many who came into contact with them were murdered or sent into exile. If you were a Senator, you had to be careful all the time. But it was difficult to know what to do. You might offend the Emperor in the Senate by saying something with which he did not agree. Or the Emperor's wife might hate you because your wife was prettier than she. One of your own enemies in the Senate might become one of the Emperor's closest friends. Whatever happened, you could in an instant lose your wealth, your family and your life. Even if you became the firm friend of one Emperor, on his death the new Emperor might hate you for this.

The most important part of Pliny's political career was spent under three Emperors: Domitian, who ruled from A.D. 81—96; Nerva, who ruled from A.D. September 96—January 98; and Trajan, who ruled from A.D. 98—117. Domitian was so hated by the Senate that he was assassinated. After his death the Senate issued a decree which ordered people to erase his name wherever it occurred throughout the empire. In the museum at Chesters near Hadrian's Wall you can see an official Roman corn measure which has had Domitian's name taken out.

Trajan, by contrast, was an Emperor the Senate loved. He became a legend. Later on, when other Senators became Emperors, the Senate used to pray 'Felicior Augusto, melior Trajano' — 'may you be luckier than Augustus was and may you be an even better Emperor than Trajan'. We can also show the contrast between these two emperors by two Roman accounts.

Domitian as Emperor

This comes from a shortened version of a history of Rome by Cassius Dio.

Domitian gives a 'party'
Domitian had one of the rooms in his palace prepared in a special way. He painted all the walls, the ceiling and the floor black. In the room he put black couches on a floor which had no carpets. Then he invited the most important Senators and **Knights** to a party. He told them to come on their own.

When they sat down on the couches, Domitian had his slaves bring in gravestones. These were put down beside each guest. Each stone had the person's own name on it. Each one also had a small oil lamp, just like you have in tombs. Then naked, handsome boys, who were painted black all over,

4

came in like ghosts. After they had danced a dance of death, one went and stood by the feet of each guest. After that more slaves brought in food on black plates and black dishes. But it was the sort of food you usually sacrifice to the dead.

All the guests thought they were going to have their throats cut any moment. They were so scared they could not say a word but they just sat there, as if they were already dead. Domitian was the only one to talk and all he could talk about was death and killing.

Then all of a sudden he sent them all home. He had each guest put in a litter and taken home by slaves they did not know. This made them even more afraid. As soon as they got home they began to get over their fears and feel better. Then there was a knock at the door and one of their own slaves announced that a messenger had come from Augustus Caesar. Everyone thought the messenger had brought an order telling them to kill themselves. But instead each messenger brought the 'gravestone' from the 'party'. These were made of silver. Then other slaves came in from the Emperor with their presents, including the cups and dishes they had used. These were made of gold and silver. The last present of all was the boy who had stood at the feet of each guest. He was now washed and in his best clothes.

Trajan as Emperor

This is part of a 'Speech of Praise', which Pliny gave in the Senate to honour the Emperor.

The Panegyricus
Every day you make us admire you more. Every day you make us love you more. You are the sort of Emperor that others could only promise to be. As time goes by you are the only one to grow in reputation and fame. You have been able to bring together two very different qualities. You have the strength of an Emperor who has ruled for a long time. You also have the willingness of a new Emperor to listen to others.

When Romans come to pay their respects to you, you do not force them to embrace your feet. And when they kiss you, you only kiss them. Your kisses and embraces are as they should be. Before you became Emperor, you used to go on foot. You still do. You used to be happy when you were working hard. You still are.

Fortune has changed everything around you but you have not changed. When you walk among us we are free. We can let you go on without us, or we can stop you, or walk beside you or go on ahead on our own. When you are with us we can do what we like. You allow us to enjoy your presence without being a do-gooder. You allow us to meet you without putting us in your debt.

Whoever comes to talk to you, can stop and talk to you. It is not your authority that makes him stop talking but his respect for you. We are ruled by you and are subjected to you. But this is just the same as being under the laws. The laws control our evil desires and evil ways, which are always part and parcel of our nature.

You stand out. You shine like Honour and Power. Honour and Power are always both way above men and somehow part of them. Other Emperors grew tired of us. They were afraid to be our equals. They couldn't walk with us. They had to be carried on the shoulders and necks of slaves, over the tops of our faces. It is fame, glory, love, and freedom that lifts you above those princes. The earth we all tread on and the footsteps you mix with ours, lift you up to the stars.

We need to be careful when we read what Roman writers say about Domitian and Trajan. Pliny wants us to believe that good men do badly under bad Emperors but get their rewards under good Emperors. 'Good men' and 'bad men' do not mean much. Domitian was a cruel tyrant but many Senators did well under him. It is a surprise to realise that Pliny is a good example. After Domitian's death, Pliny claims that his own career did not make any progress, while Domitian was Emperor. This is not true. He was Praetor and also was in charge of the Military Treasury (not a word about this in his ten books of letters). He also claims that his own life was in danger in the last weeks of Domitian's rule. Someone had informed on him and there was a letter about him among Domitian's papers. If Domitian had not been killed, Pliny might have been put on trial. We only have Pliny's own word for this and it comes when Trajan was Emperor. It does not ring true.

He also claims that he is much better off now Trajan is Emperor. When we look carefully at his career, this also does not ring quite true. He does not do as well under Trajan as he did under Domitian. He does become Consul but that was almost owed to him. He does not get an early governorship of a province, nor does he get a priesthood early. When he writes to the Emperor asking him to honour his friends, the Emperor is not all that sympathetic. The death of Domitian, whatever Pliny said when Trajan became Emperor, could well have been a serious blow to Pliny's career.

This book contains 66 letters of Pliny, which have been translated from Latin. There are ten books of letters; most of them were published in Pliny's lifetime. Scholars who have read the letters in Latin have come to different conclusions about them. Some feel that they are not real letters at all. Each letter of Pliny usually only contains one topic. Some letters do not have much detail in them. Other letters are obviously very carefully written.

While all these points are true, when we read the letters we can feel that underneath the polish and fine language they were once real letters. The problems Pliny deals with are real problems. Some of the letters read like real conversations (see letter 18). There are also parts of letters which are unclear or muddled (see the third paragraph of letter 14). Often the endings of the letters are rather scrappy (see letter 13). Even though Pliny obviously did revise the letters before he had them published, they still are rough enough in places to show they were real letters. We also know that the people Pliny wrote to were real people. They were mostly schoolfriends, family friends, local town poets and authors. Only rarely does he write to anyone of real importance.

Finally we know that Pliny was a slow worker. We are tempted to think that he wrote hundreds of letters and had only a very few published. We feel too that he must have written far more to the Emperor Trajan than we have in book X. But we just do not know. In twelve years he wrote the 9 books of letters, 14 speeches, 2 short biographies and 2 books of light verse. It does not seem a great deal. But it is when you think of all the loving care that went into revising them for publication.

A · Pliny's *'familia'*

The letters in this section are concerned with Pliny's **'familia'**. We hear about four members of his family and about his slaves and **freedmen** — all these are included in the word 'familia'. The four members of his family are: (1) His uncle, G. Plinius Secundus. He is often called Pliny the Elder, to distinguish him from our Pliny, who is known as Pliny the Younger. Pliny the Elder was a wealthy Roman Knight, who came from Comum. After the Senators, the Knights were the next important people in the Roman Empire. He had served as an officer in the army in Germany and been a **procurator** in both Africa and Spain. Procurators collected the taxes for the Emperor from his provinces. Although he had never been a Senator, he was a friend of the Emperor Vespasian and the Emperor Titus. He was in charge of the Roman fleet at Misenum when Vesuvius erupted. When he died, he adopted Pliny as his son in his will. (2) His wife, Calpurnia. She was Pliny's third and last wife, and she married him sometime between A.D. 100–104. She may only have been 14 or so, while Pliny was 40 or over. She also came from Comum from a wealthy local family. It is interesting that Pliny married her rather than some high-born lady from the city of Rome. (3) His wife's aunt, Calpurnia Hispulla. She had been responsible for bringing up Pliny's third wife. (4) The father of Hispulla and the grandfather of Calpurnia, L. Calpurnius Fabatus. As a young man he had been sent out to control six tribes in Africa. But his career had been cut short when a friend of his was accused of treason in A.D. 65. When Pliny writes to him in A.D. 104 he is an old man. It is clear from the letters that he and Pliny do not get on well with each other. He seems to have been very critical of Pliny.

Pliny's slaves and freedmen were included in his 'familia'. Although we do not know exactly how many he had, he could well have had hundreds. When the Chief of Police in

Rome was murdered by his slaves, there were 400 in his house at the time. Many of Pliny's slaves would work on his estates and have little or no contact with him. Those that acted as his servants in his house would see much more of him.

Pliny's attitude to his slaves is interesting. He sets some of them free, but even when they are freedmen, he keeps some of them living and working on for him in his house. He is also anxious and fearful of his slaves. There must have been many occasions in any day when they could have ganged up on him and killed him. We have to be careful too when we want to say that Pliny is being kind to his slaves. In law they were his possessions. He owned and could sell them just like he owned and could sell his estates and farms. When things go wrong and they become ill, he does something for them. But when you read the letters you must try and decide why he is doing what he is doing. When he sends his freedman to rest in the south of France, is he being kind to him or just having him repaired like a broken down television set?

1. My uncle

To Baebius Macer

I was very pleased to hear that you read my uncle's books with much interest. You want to get them all and you want to know how many he wrote. I will give you a list in the order in which he wrote them. This will please people like you who are interested in literature.

1. 'How to throw the Javelin, while riding a horse'. 1 volume.
   He wrote this when he was in charge of a squadron of cavalry. This book shows his great talent for writing and his great interest in the subject.
2. 'The Life of Pomponius Secundus'. 2 volumes.
   Pomponius loved my uncle as he loved no-one else. My uncle wrote this book out of duty. He wanted people to remember a fine friend.
3. 'The Wars of Germany'. 20 volumes.
   He put together all the wars we have ever had with the Germans. He began to write this when he was a soldier in

Germany. He did it because he was warned by a dream. He saw himself asleep and, as he slept, the ghost of Drusus Nero came and stood over him. Nero had defeated all of Germany far and wide but he had died there. His ghost made my uncle responsible for keeping his memory alive. He asked him to write a book to make sure he was not forgotten.

4. 'How to be a Scholar'. 3 volumes.
   There are two parts to each volume. It shows you how to be an orator and it tells you all you need to know.
5. 'Bad Grammar'. 8 volumes.
   He wrote this in the very last years of the Emperor Nero. You could not write anything else because Nero was such a difficult Emperor. You would be in trouble if you did not keep your head down.
6. 'An end to the history of Aufidius Bassus'. 31 volumes.
7. 'A Natural History'. 37 volumes.
   This has many topics and is scholarly. It is as colourful as nature herself.

You say you are amazed that a man who was so busy would write so many books with so much care. But here is something that will amaze you even more. He did all this and for a long time he still practised as a lawyer as well. He was only 55 when he died. He had spent much of the middle years of his life in the greatest offices of state and in friendship with the Emperor. He had a razor-sharp mind which he could apply wonderfully well.

He hardly needed any sleep at all. From August 23rd he used to begin to work in the night. He started then, not because he was superstitious but because he wanted to have more time for study. In the winter he would start work half-way through the night, at midnight, or one o'clock (hardly ever at two).

I know he was always very ready to drop off to sleep. He would do this, even while he was studying. One minute he would be hard at it, the next minute he would be dropping off.

While it was still dark, he would go and see the Emperor Vespasian. He was another one who worked late at night. My uncle would set out from the palace and do what he had been told to do. If there was any time left when he got home, he would get down to study again.

He was just like the good old Romans. He only ate light and easy meals in the day. If he had any free time after eating, in the summer he used to sunbathe. A slave would read him part of a book and he would make notes or copy parts out. He did this with everything. He used to say no book was wholly bad.

After he had sunbathed, his slaves would give him a cold bath. Then he would have a snack and a nap. Between teatime and dinner he would do a day's work. A slave would read a book to him over dinner and he would copy out more parts. Sometimes he did this very quickly. Once, one of his friends heard his slave read a word wrongly. He told him to go back and read the word again properly. My uncle said to his friend, 'Did you know what he meant?' 'Yes', he said. 'Well', said my uncle, 'Why did you make him go back? He could have read 10 more lines and you have stopped him.' He didn't like to lose a moment. When it was summer, he used to finish his dinner while it was still daylight. In the winter he finished eating within an hour of it getting dark. You would think he had been made to do this by law.

He did all this in the middle of the hustle and bustle of the city. When he went away for a rest to his house in the country, the only time he did not work at writing was when he was in the bath. And I do mean *in* the bath. When he was being rubbed with oil, or dried with a towel, he had a slave reading to him or he dictated some notes. When he was going from place to place, he felt he was free from his troubles. He then gave himself completely up to writing. He had a secretary at his side with a book and tablets. Even bad weather would not stop him studying and writing. In winter he wore long sleeves to protect his hands. He just wanted to write all the time. This is why he went about Rome in a litter.

I remember how he blamed me for walking. 'You cannot throw away all those hours on walking', he said. 'Any time not spent writing is a waste of time.' This is how he managed to write all those books.

He also left me 160 notebooks of extracts from books. These were written on both sides of the page and in very small writing. So they really are more than 160 notebooks.

The story goes that when he was a procurator in Spain, he could have sold them to Larcius Licinus for 400,000 **sesterces**. And at that time there were nothing like as many of them as there are today.

Think about how much he read and how much he wrote! When you do, you wouldn't have thought he had a great career in public life and had been a close friend of the Emperor. What do you feel when you hear how he worked, and worked and worked at writing? Don't you feel he had a lot more writing to do and a lot more reading to do?

I smile when others say I am keen on writing. If I compare myself to him, I am bone idle. (Well, perhaps, not that idle!) I work for the state and I work for my friends. These two things stretch me. Think of all those little men who sit their lives out, trying to write. Put them next to my uncle and wouldn't they blush! They are men who sleep and do nothing.

I only wanted to let you know how many books my uncle had written. But I have written more than I had intended. Perhaps you will like the facts about him as much as his books. They may make you read his books. They may also make you do something like him. You may even want to become his rival.

(III.5)

2. How my uncle died

To Cornelius Tacitus
You ask me to tell you how my uncle died. You want to write a really true account about him for others to read long after we are dead. I thank you for writing to me. If you write about his death, you will keep his memory alive forever. I know this very well.

My uncle died in a disaster that struck one of the most lovely parts of the world. He will live on and he will be remembered because of that. But disasters like that are remembered because they happen to cities and people. My uncle had also stored away many things of his own which he had written. These will last a long time. Even so you write books that last forever, and if you write about him, so will he.

Men who are blessed, get one of two gifts from the gods. They do deeds that must be written about. Or they write books that must be read. If you do both, you are the most blessed among the blessed. My uncle will be one of these, because of his books and yours. So I am very willing to help you. No! I must say more. I demand that you write about my uncle.

My uncle was in charge of the Roman fleet at Misenum. About two o'clock on August 24th my mother showed me a cloud which was very big and looked odd. My uncle had spent his day as usual. He had been sunbathing, had taken a cold bath and had his lunch. He was now studying, when he heard about the cloud. He called a slave to fetch his shoes, climbed up a hill and got the best view he could of the mystery.

The cloud was getting bigger and it had a flat head, like a Mediterranean Pine tree. It was carried up into the air on a very long trunk which broke into branches. The trunk was made by the blast from the volcano pushing up hard. As it got higher into the atmosphere, the blast was less strong and the ash got heavier and began to fan out. The cloud sometimes glowed white hot, sometimes the earth and ash in it made it dirty and blotchy. For a long time we did not know which mountain it was coming from. It was only later we found it was Vesuvius.

My uncle, who was a great scholar, just could not keep away. He ordered a fast boat and asked me if I would like to go with him. He had just given me some writing to do, and so I told him I wanted to study. As he was leaving the house, he had a message from Rectina, the wife of Tascus. She was terrified by the danger, because her villa was at the foot of the mountain and she could only get away by boat. She begged my uncle to snatch her away from the danger. This made him change his mind. He had started out only out of curiosity, to see what was going on. But he went on to do something heroic.

He ordered all the warships to be launched and he went on one himself. He wanted to help everyone, not only Rectina. You see, because the place was so pleasant, it was full of people. While others were hurrying away from the town, he was hurrying to it. He sailed right into the middle of the danger.

As he sailed to the town, he made careful observations. He took notes of everything that was going on. You can see how

13

unafraid he was. When they got near Pompeii, the ashes were hotter and fell more thickly. They were also hit by pumice and stones. These had been burned black and broken into pieces by the fires. All of a sudden they sailed into the shallows, which were full of debris from the volcano. For a moment my uncle stopped and thought he might turn back. When the helmsman said he should, he replied, 'Fortune favours the fearless. Sail round to the villa of Pomponianus!'

Pomponianus had a villa at Stabiae, where the sea comes into the bay along a gentle curve. He could only get away by sea and was now cut off. Even so, although he could see what might happen to him, he was not at that moment in any real danger.

When the danger did get near, Pomponianus put all his goods into ships and was ready to escape, if only the wind would let him. But the ships could not get away because the wind was blowing from the sea onto the land.

The wind helped my uncle's ship to get there very quickly. My uncle greeted Pomponianus, told him not to worry and cheered him up. He wanted to get rid of his friend's fear by showing how calm he was. So he ordered the bath to be made ready for him. After his bath, he lay down and had dinner. He was happy or he looked happy. And that was as good as being happy.

While they were having their dinner, huge sheets of flame shot up all over the place and great walls of fire flashed in answer to them. When it got dark, the fire and flames seemed brighter than ever.

My uncle kept on saying that the peasants had got into a panic and left their fires burning in the fields. Or he said the only houses which were burning were those that had been deserted and abandoned. He said all this to stop Pomponianus being terrified. Then he went off to bed and slept very soundly. He was a heavy man and rather stout. Because of this, he was a heavy breather. The slaves who guarded his bedroom, heard him fast asleep. After a while the yard in front of his room got filled with ash and pumice. If he had stopped there any longer he would not have been able to get out of the room.

When the slaves woke him up, he came out and came back to Pomponianus and the others. They had not slept at all. They then all discussed what to do. Should they stop in the house or wander off in the open?

14

By now the houses were shaking with the huge tremors. These were coming thick and fast. Buildings were being torn from their foundations and seemed to sway backwards and forwards. If my uncle and his friend went outside, they felt they would be hurt by falling pumice, even though this was light and hollow.

In the end they decided not to stop indoors. All the others wanted to get outside because with them one fear got the better of their other fears. My uncle was the only one who let one good reason get the better of other good reasons. So they put pillows on their heads and tied them on with cloths to protect themselves. In every other part of the world it was day. In Pompeii it was the blackest of black nights. Those who were left in the city, only got rid of the dark by torches and all sorts of lamps.

My uncle decided to go out onto the shore and see for himself if the sea would let them sail. But it was still angry and against them. His slaves put down a sheet for him to lie on and he demanded and drank one or two cups of cold water. Then the flames and the smell of sulphur, which always tells you the flames are coming, made the others run away. These flames made him wake up. He stood up, leaning on two young slaves, but he fell down straight away. I suppose the thick fumes had blocked his windpipe and closed his gullet which was always weak and giving him trouble. When they found his body in the light two days later, there was not a mark on it. He still had his clothes on. He looked like a man who was having a rest, not a man who had died.

My mother and I were as Misenum and — but I won't bother you with us. You are writing history and you wanted to know how he died. So I will stop there. I have put down in full everything I had a part in and everything I heard at the time. I have done this very carefully. You use what you think best. It is one thing to write a letter. It is another thing to write history. It is one thing to write for a friend. It is another thing to write for the world.

(VI.16)

(See page 78 for a different account of the eruption of Vesuvius.)

15

3. How much my wife loves me

To Calpurnia Hispulla

You show us all how we should love our own family. Your
brother was a fine man. You loved him as much as he loved
you. You now love his daughter as if she were your own. You
are not only an aunt to her but also a father.

You will be pleased to know that she is a credit to her
father, to you and to her grandfather. She is very sharp and
very careful. I am the only man she loves and that shows you
what sort of girl she is. She also likes reading literature. She
has got this from me. She has all my books which she reads.
She has also learnt them by heart.

You should see her when I am about to go to court. How
worried she is! When I have finished speaking there, how
pleased she is. She sends slaves out into the city. They fly
back and tell her how I have got on. She wants to know how
often I was clapped and how I won the day.

If I invite my friends to a **reading**, she sits and listens
behind a curtain. When they clap me, she laps up the applause.
She has even set some of my poems to music and plays them
on the lyre. Love, which is the best teacher in the world, has
made her do this. No one else has forced her.

This is why I am sure our happiness will grow as the days
go by and last for ever. She is not in love with me as I am nor
with my body. This will grow old and weak as time goes by.
She loves me for what I stand for. This is just what I would
expect from someone who has been educated by your hands.
She has been trained in your camp and she sees only what is
holy and honest.

No wonder she has come to love me as you said she would.
For you always looked upon my mother as your mother.
Even when I was small, it was you who guided me. It was you
who praised me. You knew the sort of person I would be. So
each of us fall over each other to thank you. I, because you
gave her to me, and she because you gave me to her. You
would think we had chosen each other.

(IV.19)

4. To his wife who is ill

To Calpurnia

I have never complained so much about having too much to do. You are off to Campania to get better and I cannot come because I have too much to do. I cannot even join you later.

I really wanted to be with you to see for myself how you are getting on. I wanted to see how your strength was improving. I want to know what you are taking for it. Campania is a tempting place. I hope you avoid temptation.

Even if you were strong and healthy, I would love you and miss you. It is terrible not to have news of someone you love most deeply. You are away from me and you are ill. These are two good reasons why I am anxious. I am afraid of everything. I invent all sorts of things happening to you. That is what you do when you are afraid. I think the worst things that can happen to you, are going to happen to you.

So I ask and beg you. Write to me at least once or twice a day and banish my fear. You see, when I am reading your letters, I feel well. It is only when I have finished reading them, I begin to be afraid again.

(VI.4)

5. What his wife's letters do to Pliny

To Calpurnia

You say you miss me very much. My books which you keep close to you, are the only things that give you any comfort. It is nice to know that you miss us and that you get some comfort from my books.

For my part, I read your letters again and again. I pick them up as if they had just come. They make me burn with desire for you all the more. I know your letters are pure pleasure but to talk to you face to face is sheer delight.

Write to me as often as you can. If you do, you will thrill me and torture me, both at once.

(VI.7)

6. Pliny writes a love letter

To Calpurnia

You cannot know how much I miss you. First of all because I love you. Secondly, because we are not used to being away from each other. Most of the night I am wide awake and you are with me. In the day I am drawn to your room at the times when I used to visit you. Then I trail back to my own room, sick and sad. I am like a lover with no rivals, who has had the door slammed in his face.

The only time I am let off the rack is when I am worn out in the Forum or the law courts. I only find peace of mind in trouble. I only find my comfort in the misery and problems of others. What sort of life do you think that is?

(VII.5)

7. Bad news

To Calpurnia Hispulla, the aunt of his wife

I know how you love your niece. You are even kinder to her than a mother would be. So I shall tell you first what I ought to tell you last. Then you will be happy. Even so I fear that you will first of all be pleased. Then you will become afraid.

Anyway, be happy your niece is out of danger. You will, of course, be horrified to hear that her life has been in danger. She is now cheerful. She has come back to me from the dead and she is getting better. But the stronger she gets, the more you realise how ill she has been. She almost died and it was not her own fault. She only did what any girl of her age might do. That is why she had a miscarriage.

So you cannot take comfort for the death of your brother in the birth of a grandnephew or niece. But we shall have a child even though it is not to be now. And your niece, who can give us one, is safe. Please explain what has happened to your father. Women do understand these things much better than men.

(VIII.11)

8. Silly girl

To Calpurnius Fabatus, his wife's grandfather

Because I know how much you want to have a great-grandchild, I know too you will be all the more sad to hear our news. Your granddaughter has had a miscarriage and lost the child. She really is only a girl and did not even know she was pregnant. She did not do what all pregnant women should do. Instead she did what she should not have done and now she has paid for her foolishness by very nearly losing her life.

This news must upset you. You must feel that you have been robbed in your old age of heirs, who were all ready to be born. Even so disappointed though you are, you must thank the gods. I know they have not yet given you children to carry on the family name. But they have kept your granddaughter alive and they will give you children in the future.

Things have not worked out right this time. Yet the fact that your granddaughter can have children, shows that one day she will have children. This is what I say to myself and this is what I say to you. You cannot wish harder for children than I do. With their background they should have a splendid start in public life. They will take with them our names which are well known and the reputation of our family. If they can only just come along, then they will turn our night into day.

(VIII.10)

9. What a generous man you are

To Calpurnius Fabatus

Thank you for your letter. You say you have dedicated a splendid colonnade and had your own name and your son's name put on it. On the next day you promised the money to decorate the doors. This new gift finished off the first one nicely. How generous you are.

I am pleased because this makes you more famous. Part of that fame comes down to me because you are my wife's grandfather. I am also pleased because I see a splendid building which keeps alive the memory of my father-in-law. Last of all I am pleased because our home town is doing so well. I know this is the thing that makes you very happy.

19

I have only one more thing to say. I hope the gods will always keep you so generous. May they give you many years to use that generosity. Now that you have done what you have promised, you will begin on something else. Someone who is as generous as you, does not know when to stop. Beauty is made to shine when it is used.

(V.11)

10. Pliny has made his wife's grandfather angry

To Calpurnius Fabatus

You should not hesitate to commend to me people who must have my help. You think it right to help many people. I think it right to help you out with anything that affects you. So I shall give Bittius Priscus as much help as I can, especially in the battlefield I know best, the **Centumviral Court**.

You order me to forget the letters in which you told me exactly what you thought of me. But they are just the ones I love to remember. They make me feel how much you love me. You criticise me like you criticised your own son.

I also must say this. I was all the more pleased to have you say exactly what you felt, because I was in the right. I had been very careful to be careful over this because this is what you said you wanted. So I ask you again and again. If I seem to let you down (I say 'seem' because I never in fact shall ever let you down), tell me off with that same rough frankness. If you do, we shall both learn something. I shall know you are doing it because you really love me. And you will be happy to find out that I did not deserve what you said about me.

(VI.12)

11. Pliny backs up his freedman

To Calpurnius Fabatus

You are surprised to hear that Hermes, my freedman has sold some land to Corellia. This was land which I inherited and was part of an estate. The person who left the land, gave half of it to me and the rest to some other people.

I did not want the land to be sold at a public auction. So I ordered my freedman to sell it. He thought my half of the estate was worth 700,000 sesterces. You say it is worth 900,000 and you think I have lost 200,000 sesterces. You now ask me if I am going to stick with what my freedman has done.

Well, I am. And here are the reasons why. You and those who were left part of the estate must excuse me, because I had to obey a higher call. I am not in the same position as them. My duty to Corellia must come first. She is the sister of Corellius Rufus and I hold his memory sacred. Secondly she was my own mother's best friend. Also I know her husband, Minicius Iustus very well. He is a very good man. I am even more friendly with his son. He actually presided at my Games, when I was praetor.

When I last came to see you, Corellia told me she would like to buy some land by the side of Lake Como. I said she could have anything she liked of mine except for the land which my parents left me. That is the one thing I could not let her have. I also said she could fix her own price. Then luck gave me this inheritance which contained that piece of land. So I wrote to Corellia and told her I wanted to sell it to her. Hermes took the letter and when she ordered him to let her have the land there and then, he obeyed.

I must confirm what my freedman has done because he is my freedman, and he was following my wishes. I am sure you will understand this. Those who were left part of the estate with me, may be angry, because I sold separately some land which I need not have sold at all. But no-one is making them do what I have done. They do not have the same duty to Corellia. They can look after themselves. I had to look after a *friend*.

(VII.11)

12. One of my freedmen is ill

To Valerius Paulinus

I see how kind you are to those who serve you. I can now tell you how fond I am of those who serve me. I can never forget that quotation from Homer, 'how mild he was as a father'. Nor can I forget what we Romans mean when we talk about being the 'Father of a family'. By nature I do not think I am too hard-hearted or too tough. But even if I were, I would be shattered by the illness of my freedman. He must have all the kindness he can be given. As a person, he is honest, dutiful and artistic. I put him down in my account books as a 'comoedus'. And he is very good at it.

He speaks in a lively way. There is a wisdom in what he says, and he speaks to the point. There is also something attractive about him. He can play the lyre with a skill that a comoedus does not need. He can read speeches, parts of histories, or poems with such a skill that you would think that he had been specially trained to do only this. I have been careful to give you these details so that you can understand just how many services that one man provides for me. You will also realise how pleasantly he does them. My love for him goes a long way back. It has now become all the greater because of the danger to him. Nothing makes your love grow more than when you are afraid of losing something that you love.

That seems to be what everyone would feel in a situation like this. And I myself have been through all this before with him. Some years ago, when he was acting, he strained himself and spat up blood. Because of this he was sent by me to Egypt. He stayed there a long time, recovered and has recently got back. But now he has been using his voice too much and for too long. He has brought up some more blood, although he was warned by a little cough that his old illness was back.

This is the reason why I have decided to send him to your estates at **Forum Iulii**. I have often heard you talk about them. The air there is refreshing and the milk perfect for treating that sort of problem. I ask you please to write to your servants to open up the house for him. They should also cover any expenses he may have. But knowing him, he will not have many. He is by nature thrifty. He is so careful that he denies himself not only luxuries but also essentials to his own cure. As he sets out, I will give him enough money for the journey to bring him into your care.

(V.19)

13. Slaves, death and the baths

To Acilius

Something terrible has happened. I can tell you something about it in a letter but it needs more than this.

Larcius Makedo, a man who had already been praetor, has been killed by his slaves. He was a proud and cruel master. His father had been a slave. Perhaps he remembered that too little or perhaps too much.

Anyway he was being bathed in his house in the country. Suddenly the slaves close in on him. One slave goes for his throat, another smashes him in the face, a third slave hits him in his chest, in his stomach and in his crotch. That's a terrible thing to have to say.

When they think he is dead, they drop him on to the very hot floor of the baths. They wanted to test whether he had any life in him. Makedo was unconscious or pretended to be. So he lay there, not moving at all, just like a dead man.

The slaves carry him out of the bath as if he had fainted. Other slaves, more faithful ones, take him over. While this is going on, the **concubinae**, which Makedo kept in the house, ran together shouting and making a great din. Their voices and the coldness outside brought him back to life. He opened his eyes, moved himself, shook his limbs and showed that he was alive. You see, it was now safe for him to do this.

All the slaves ran away. Most of them have been recaptured and the rest are being looked for. For a few days Makedo got better, but then he died. And there is something unusual about his death. Most masters, when they are killed by their slaves, do not know if they are going to be avenged. Makedo did.

You can see how we live in danger from our slaves. You can see how our slaves abuse us. You can see how our slaves play deadly games with us. Even if you are a master who is kind and gentle, you still have to worry. Slaves always have two sides to their nature. They act with reason like men. They also act by instinct like animals. It is when their instincts get the better of them that they kill their masters.

Well, that's enough of that! What else is new? Nothing or I would have let you know. But as I have got some space left and I am on holiday, I'll add a little more about Makedo.

When he was being bathed in the Great Baths at Rome, something happened that should have warned him off baths. One of Makedo's own slaves touched a Roman **Knight**. He wanted to ask him to let his master get by. The Knight turned round and hit out. But he missed the slave and hit Makedo. He hit him so hard that he knocked him to the ground. So you see, Makedo ought to have been more careful about baths. First of all they were the place where he was abused. Then they were the place where he was killed.

(III.14)

14. If I am ill . . .

To Geminus

I am frightened because you are always ill. I know you are a very sensible man but I am afraid you may change. So I give you this piece of advice. Be patient and fight the illness. If you do this, others will praise you and you will get well. This is certainly possible.

Here is something I say to my 'familia' when I am well. 'If ever I am seriously ill, I do not want to have anything which I will later regret or be ashamed of. If a disease gets hold of me, I want you not to give me anything without the permission of the doctors. But, also, be sure I shall punish you if you do. Other people punish their slaves for not giving them what they wanted. I am not like them.'

I was burnt up some time ago by a raging fever. When it was going away and I had been oiled for the bath, I was offered something to drink by the doctor. I held out my hand and told him to take my pulse. Then I gave him back the cup which he had put to my lips. Later, on the 20th day of the illness, when I was being made ready for the bath, I saw the doctors mumbling among themselves. I asked the reason why. They said I could have a bath but there was some risk. 'What is the point, then, of having a bath?' I said. And so calmly and with no fuss I forgot all about the joys of having a bath, even though in my imagination I was as good as in it.

I made up my mind to show the same calm attitude to not having a bath as I did before to having one. And I did show it!

I sent you this story about myself to illustrate my advice

to you. Now I have shown you what a model of good behaviour I am. I shall have to keep that way in the future. This letter will keep me on the straight and narrow path.

(VII.1)

15. Death on the road to Rome

To Hispanus
You tell me Robustus, a distinguished Roman Knight, went as far as Ocriculum with Atilius Scaurus, a friend of mine. Then he disappeared. You would like Scaurus to see if he can find any trace of him. He will come to look but it may not do any good. I suspect the same thing has happened to him as happened to Metilius Crispus, who came from Comum. I had got him promoted to the rank of centurion. When he went off from here to Rome, I gave him 40,000 sesterces. He was going to buy his uniform and fit himself out. But after he had gone, I never had a letter from him. Nor did I hear that he had died. No one knows if he was cut down by his slaves or killed with them. He was not seen again. His slaves were not seen again. Nor have any of Robustus' slaves been found.

Let us see what we can do. Let us send for Scaurus. We owe this to your family. We owe this to the most sincere efforts of that splendid young man who is looking for the father he has lost. I see how careful and how shrewd he is, in doing this. The gods have already helped him find the one man who went with his father on part of his journey. May the gods bless him with success again.

(VI.25)

16. When slaves die

To Paternus
I have been worn out by the sickness or death of my slaves, especially if they are young. But I find comfort in two things and they are a real comfort. First of all, it is easy to give some of them their freedom. When I set slaves free, I do not think of them as dying before their time. Secondly I let those who die as slaves make a will. Of course it is not a real 'legal' will.

It cannot be, because they are slaves and cannot own anything. I 'own' them. But I treat these 'wills' as if they were real wills. They instruct me and ask me to do what they want. I follow their instructions just as if I really had been told to do so by the law. So they divide out what they have got, they make gifts and leave things. I do not mind so long as it is all kept within my 'familia'. The house is a sort of commonwealth and makes them feel like citizens.

These two things comfort me and give me some peace. But even so, I am weakened and shattered by the very feelings for humanity which made me act like this in the first place. However I do not want to seem to become more hard-hearted. There are men who do not see the death of a slave as a misfortune. They see it only as good money lost down the drain. They see themselves as men who are great and men who are wise. They may be great and wise. But men they are not! A real man does grieve, has feelings, can fight them, lets someone comfort him and really needs to be comforted. But perhaps I have said more than I ought to have done on this. It is still less than what I wanted to say. You can get real pleasure out of grief, especially if you weep with a friend. Friends are ready to praise you or at least pardon you for the tears you shed.

(VIII.16)

17. Pliny wants a doctor to become a Roman citizen

To Trajan, the Emperor

Master, I was seriously ill last year and nearly lost my life. I had a doctor of ointments to see me. He was very careful and showed great concern. I can only pay back what I owe him by a gift which you alone can give. I ask you, please make him a Roman citizen. He is a **peregrinus** and was given this status by a peregrinus. He is called Arpocras and his patron who is now dead, was called Thermuthis.

I also ask you to grant Roman citizenship to Hedia and Antonia Harmeris, freedwomen of the most noble lady, Antonia Maximilla. She has asked me to ask you.

(X.5)

18. Getting a teacher for Comum

To Cornelius Tacitus

I am glad that you have got to the city safe and sound. Everyone else no doubt wants to see you but so do I most of all. I must however stay on only a few more short days in my villa here in Tusculum. I have a little job on my hands that I want to finish. I know if I don't finish it now, it will never get done.

When I do see you, there is something I want to ask you but I'll make a start on it now. I am in a hurry and want to get a move on with it. First of all I'll tell you why I am asking you a favour. Then I'll tell you what the favour is.

When I went to my home town the other week, the young son of a citizen came to pay his respects to me. I said to him,

'Do you go to school?'

'Yes.'

'Where?'

'Milan.'

'Why do you not go here?'

His father who was with him said, 'Because we don't have any teachers.' There were many other fathers who happened to be listening as well. 'Why don't you have any?' said I. 'You fathers ought to know how important it is that your children should study here rather than anywhere else. Their own town is the most pleasant place for them to be. In their own town they can be properly brought up under the very eyes of their parents. It also costs less. It doesn't take much to set up a fund and hire some teachers. Pay them what you now spend on lodgings, fares to and from Milan, and all the other things the children have to buy because they are not at home. When you are not at home, you have to buy everything. No, I'll go further. You know that I do not have any children of my own but I think of our town as a daughter or a parent. I am willing to give you a third of whatever money you raise.'

I would have promised to give them all of it but I was afraid someone one day would take advantage of my generosity. I see this happening everywhere where teachers are hired by towns, and there is only one remedy for it. Parents must be the only ones with the right to hire teachers. If they have to find the money to pay teachers, they will be careful to choose good ones. Some men are not careful with other people's money but they are if it is their own. And if they are careful over their own money, they will be careful with mine. This is the way to get good teachers.

So I said to them, 'Make up your minds to do this and work for it. Follow the lead I have given you. I want to give you as much as I can. You couldn't do anything better for your children. You could not do anything which would please the Fatherland more. Let those who are born here, be educated here. While they are still very young let them come to love the land that gave them birth. Let them fill it out.

'Wouldn't it be great if you hired teachers who were first class? Then other towns might want to join in our studies, and instead of your children going to some foreign place, the foreigners would flock here.'

I thought I had better begin at the beginning and give you the full story. I want you to know how grateful I will be if you do me this favour. You can see how important it is. Anyway, this is what I want to ask you. You have a large number of students who come to see you because they admire you so much. Can you look at them carefully and find any that we can interview? Please note that I am not offering them a teaching post. I leave all that to the parents. Let them be the judges and let them choose the teachers. All I want to do is to see that it is done properly and the money is spent wisely. So if there is someone who thinks he is good enough, let him come here, but only on this condition. The only thing he can be confident of is the confidence he brings with himself.

(IV.13)

19. How to do the town some good

To Caninius
You want me to give you some advice. You want to put some money aside for a feast for the citizens of Comum. You are not sure how this money can be kept safe and properly used on their behalf when you are in your grave. You do me an honour by asking for my advice but it is difficult for me to answer.

You could put aside a large sum of money and give it to

the Town Council. But they might squander it. This is what I fear most. So you must be very careful about this.

Or you could buy some land and you could give the land to the town. But the town does not look after properly the things it owns.

Or you could do what I have done. I promised to give the town 500,000 sesterces. I wanted the money to help look after free-born boys and girls. But I did not trust the town to use it properly. So I sold some of my land, which was worth more than 500,000 sesterces, to the Town Clerk. He put a rent on it and rented it back to me for 30,000 a year.

If you do it this way, the town is all right and they have no problems about getting the money. And, because the land is so good and the rent so small, there will always be people wanting to rent it. I know I have spent a good deal more than 500,000 sesterces because the rent fixed at 30,000 a year has brought down the market price of very good land. But you must put the town first and not yourself. You must do something for tomorrow, when you will not be here, and not for today, when you are here. You must also be far more careful over making a gift than making a profit.

(VII.18)

B · Public life

Pliny was a man who spent a good deal of his life making speeches in public. Apart from being an author and a financial expert he was also well known as a lawyer. He practised law very often in the Centumviral Court in Rome, which dealt with disputes over wills and inheritances. It was here that he came into rivalry with M. Aquilius Regulus. We get little impression from Pliny of how influential and important a man Regulus had been. Although Pliny treats him with a certain contempt, Regulus had been a remarkable man. His father had been ruined and sent into exile. Regulus while still a young man had made his name as a speaker by successfully prosecuting three men who had been Consuls and seeing them condemned to death. The Emperor Nero rewarded him handsomely for this with a priesthood, made him a quaestor and gave him a fortune in money. Under the Emperor Domitian he had become the most influential lawyer in the Centumviral Court. Being able to speak well enough in court to get others condemned was one sure way of getting on in Roman politics. Pliny admits in one of his other letters that he had thought about doing just that himself. He says, 'When Domitian was killed, I felt that here was a great opportunity for me to attack the guilty, to avenge those who had suffered and to advance my own career.'

Pliny also spoke often in the Senate. The highlights of his career here were when he took part in five great trials of Senators who were being prosecuted for misgovernment. Pliny helped prosecute three of them and defended the other two. It was also in the Senate that he delivered his 'Speech of Honour' to the Emperor.

From Pliny's letters we get a curious picture of the Senate. Once it had been the great governing body of Rome, making real decisions, free and subject only to itself. In Pliny's day, despite the new freedom after Domitian's death, everything depended on the Emperor. If you read the trial of Marius Priscus (see letter 25) carefully, you will notice how the Senators in the end all do what the people round the Consuls' chairs do. Pliny does not mention this but one of the Consuls was the Emperor.

The picture we get of the Senate is not very impressive. The five great trials are really something rare. Generally it discusses matters of much less importance. Even here sometimes the Senators show they do not know what the proper procedure should be in dealing with a point of law. They also fail to suppress bribery, cannot even hold their own elections decently and spend a good deal of time on what seem trivial matters, like the problem of a market in a small town in northern Italy (see letter 27).

20. A man Pliny does not like

To Calvisius

Have your money ready and prepare yourself for a golden story. No, this story has reminded me of two more so I'll tell you three. And it doesn't matter which one I tell first.

Verania, the wife of Piso, was lying in bed very ill. Regulus, bold as brass, comes to see her. What a cheek the man has! As you know Verania's husband could not stand Regulus at all. Anyway, it would have been bad enough if he had just come to call. But no! He sits himself down beside her and asks her what was the day, what was the hour, when she was born. When she tells him, he arranges his face, fixes his eyes, moves his lips, counts on his fingers and does some sums. And then he shuts up.

When he had the poor woman almost dying of suspense, he said, 'You are going through a most dangerous period. But you will come out of the wood alive. Just to confirm my view I will go and see the **haruspex** I often use.' Not a moment is lost. He makes a sacrifice and says that the entrails of the animal agrees with the forecast of the stars. The poor lady believes him and thinks she is in danger. So she calls for her will and puts Regulus down for a large sum of money. Soon she gets worse and, as she dies, she shouts that there is no bigger cheat and liar than Regulus. He had sworn an oath that all would be well, when it wasn't and he had sworn the oath on the life of his own son. This is just typical of Regulus. He is always doing this sort of wicked thing. He invites the anger of the gods to fall not on himself but on his unlucky son.

Here is the second story. Velleius Blaesus was a rich man who had been Consul. In his last illness, he wanted to change his will. Regulus who had started to work on him, hoped to get something out of the new will. So he asked the doctors to keep Blaesus alive by whatever way they could. After the new will was all signed and sealed, Regulus changed his tune. He said to the doctors, 'What is the point of torturing this poor man? You cannot make him better. Why don't you let him die and be happy?' So Blaesus dies but he didn't leave Regulus a sausage. You would have thought he had heard everything Regulus said.

Here is the third story. Aurelia, a noble lady, had put her best clothes on because she was about to sign her will. Regulus came to the ceremony. When he saw her, he said, 'Please when you die, leave me what you are wearing.' Aurelia thought he was joking but he was not. Regulus made her open up the tablets on which the will was written. Then she had to write that Regulus was to have what she was wearing. He also watched her carefully and checked to see she had written it correctly. He made her do this as if she was on her death bed. Luckily she is still alive.

What a man Regulus is! He accepts inheritances. He accepts legacies. And all as if he really deserved them. But why do I get all hot and bothered because I live in a city where the bad do better than the good? Look at Regulus. He has gone from being poor and lowly to being very well off. And it is all because he is bad. He is a great believer in trying to predict the future. For instance, one day he was looking at the entrails of an animal he had sacrificed. He wanted to see if he would be worth 60 million sesterces. He found the animal had two sets of entrails. So he thought he would soon be worth 120 million. You see, he can make other people write in their wills things they don't want to.

(II.20)

32

21. Regulus' son dies

To Attius Clemens

Regulus has lost his son. This was the only thing he did not deserve. But perhaps he would not think it so bad.

The boy was quite sharp but you could not rely on him. He could have been honest if he had not been like his father. Regulus used the law to catch the boy. He set him free from his own legal power as a father so that the boy could inherit what his mother had left him. When the boy was legally free, he got him back in his clutches by pretending to be a fond and loving parent. This was a most disgusting and sickening business. Parents who love their children do not do that. You would not believe it but remember we are talking about Regulus.

The boy is now dead and he mourns for him like a lunatic. He had many pets — ponies, dogs, nightingales, parrots and blackbirds. When the boy was about to be cremated, Regulus had all these killed around the pyre. That is not the sort of thing a father does when he is hurt because his own son has died. All Regulus did was to show off.

But no-one now can keep away from Regulus. It's amazing. They all hate him. They all can't stand him. But they flock round him, just as if they liked him, just as if they loved him. They imitate him and that is the highest form of flattery.

Regulus keeps himself in his gardens across the River Tiber. He has bought up a great area of land and filled it with huge colonnades. He has also filled up all the river bank with statues of himself. He is both very mean and a great spender. He is both wicked and a great boaster. In this way he annoys the state at a most unhealthy time. And because he annoys it, he thinks he gets some comfort for his sorrow.

Now he says he wants to find someone to marry, but like everything else, he is only saying it. You will soon hear talk in the city of the marriage of an old man who has lost a son. If a man marries while he is mourning the death of a son, he does so too early. If a man marries when he is too old, he does so too late.

How do I know he will marry? Not from anything he has

said, because he is the biggest liar out. I know because he will always do what he ought not to do.

(IV.2)

22. How determined Regulus is

To Catius Lepidus
You often say what a strong will Regulus has. It is amazing what he can do when he makes up his mind. He decided to mourn his son and he did so in a way that no-one else has done. He had as many statues and busts of his son made as he could. He had these made at each and every workshop in the city. He has this one in colours, that one in wax, another in bronze, others in gold, ivory and marble.

He also wrote a life of his son and he read it out to a large audience that he had invited. Fancy writing a speech about a boy! But he read it out all the same. Then he had a thousand copies made and sent them throughout the whole of Italy and the provinces. He has written a letter to go with it for all to read. In this letter he has invited the city councils to choose the councillor with the best reading voice to read the speech out to all the people. All this has been done. I wish he had used his strong will to do something better. Think how much good he might have done.

Good men are not as determined as bad men. When you do not know about something, there is nothing you do not try. That is what bad men do. When you stop and think, what happens is you think and stop! That is what good men do. Because good men hesitate, they find they cannot take any action. With bad men, it is different. The idea of doing something big, bold and bad makes them do it.

Regulus is a good example of a bad man. He tries to be an orator. But he does not know how to breathe properly. You cannot hear what he says. He stammers. He is slow at finding the right word. He cannot remember a thing. When he wants to act, he has to do something bad. But he is so determined to be an orator, that people think he is an orator.

An orator should be 'a good man who speaks well'. But if by 'orator' you mean 'a bad man, who does not know how to speak well', then Regulus is an orator.

34

Send me a letter and pay me back for writing to you. You will pay me back if you write and say you have seen Regulus' speech. I can see it now being read aloud by some clown at the fair. 'Step right up, ladies and gentlemen, and hear all about the death of Regulus' son.' You would want to laugh, not cry.

You would also think the speech was written *by* a child, not *about* one.

(IV.7)

23. Regulus had some good qualities

To Arrianus

There are times when I look for M. Regulus in court. I look for him but I don't want to say I miss him. Why do I look for him? He thought literature very important. When he spoke in court, his fear showed in his face. He used to go deathly pale. He also took the trouble to write everything down before he spoke, even though he could not recite it from memory. He used eye shadow. If he was defending someone, he would put it on his left eye. If he was attacking someone, he would put it on his right. He had a white patch which he changed over from eyebrow to eyebrow. He also consulted the haruspex, to see if he would win his cases. He did all this because he was so superstitious. But it also showed he loved the law courts.

He did something else too which pleased any lawyer appearing in the same case as he. He asked to be allowed to speak for as long as he wanted. He also drew people to come and listen to him. Think of it! Being able to speak as long as you like and someone else getting the blame, because it was his idea.

That is enough of that. Regulus did well to die. He could have done better if he had died sooner. If he was alive today, he would not be causing as much trouble. Our good **Princeps** would see to that. So I suppose it is right that we look for him. After he died, lawyers have had less and less time to speak in cases. In some cases we are only allowed 20 minutes. All some lawyers now want to do is to get finished, rather than get started. The judges want to get away rather than give a verdict which they have properly considered. No-one gives a damn. No-one does a thing. No-one bothers about writing and speaking in public. They do not realise how dangerous it will be for everyone, if there aren't any more good lawyers.

Or have I got it wrong? When our ancestors heard cases they gave them time and let them be postponed. They did this all the time. Are we wiser than they? Are we more just than their laws? I suppose they were stupid, too slow to catch a cold. Of course, we speak more clearly than they did. Of course, our brains work faster. Of course, we can judge cases more carefully because we rush through them. We close our cases in the time it took them to open theirs. When Regulus wanted as much time as possible, he was thinking only about himself. It is a sad thing. Few lawyers today want more time even for their own clients.

When I am acting as a judge now — and at the present time I do this more often than I act as a lawyer — I let the lawyers have all the time they want. It is silly to fix in advance how long a case will take, when it has not been heard. It is silly to put a limit on a trial when you do not know how important it may be. A judge must have one great quality. He must have patience. Patience is a great part of justice.

Of course there are problems with letting lawyers speak as long as they want to. They say all sorts of things that have nothing to do with the case. This is true. But it is better that they do say those rather than leave out things which are important. And how can you tell they have nothing to do with the case unless you have heard them? I will tell you about this and the other things that are wrong with our state when I meet you. You love our land dearly and have a strong wish to alter those things that cannot now be put right.

Finally, how are things at home? Is all going well? I am pleased with the blessings that are still with me. My own problems seem less because I have learned to live with them.

(VI.2)

24. Life is full of ups and downs

To Fabius Valens
I was speaking the other day to all four sections of the Cen-

tumviral Court when I remembered I had done this before as
a young man. I let my thoughts ramble. I began to think of
all the men who had spoken with me in that court when I
was young. Now I was the only one left. All the rest had been
struck down by Luck or Life. Good luck can turn to bad, life
turns to death. Some of my friends are dead, others are in
exile. One cannot come because he is old and not well.
Another has given up work and has retired. He wanted to do
this and he is very happy. One is a general in the army.
Another one is working for our Princeps and is far too busy
for this sort of work.

When I think of myself, I see how everything has changed
with me. I got on and did well because I worked hard to be a
good public speaker. When I became a good speaker I got
into serious trouble. Now I am back on the way up. Good
men have helped me. Good men have done me harm. Now
good men are helping me again. All this has happened in a
very short time. But if you add up how many times my luck
has changed, this 'short time' is a lifetime of experience.

This all goes to show you must not give up hope. Nothing
will stay the same for ever. Life has so many ups and downs.
I am sharing these thoughts with you because I think of you
as one of my 'familia'. I give you the same advice as I give
myself. That is why I wrote this letter.

(IV.24)

25. The case of Marius Priscus

To Arrianus
You have retired from public life because you love peace and
quiet. Even so you still care about the good name of Rome. I
know you are always very happy to hear about anything
which brings credit to the Senate. Let me tell you what has
just happened. It was to do with someone very important. It
is an example of sternness that will do us all some good.
Because it was so important, it will last forever.

The Africans accused Marius Priscus of taking bribes when
he was their governor. Marius did not bother to defend himself but he pleaded guilty. He then asked the Senate to appoint

judges to decide how much he should pay back. The Senate asked myself and Cornelius Tacitus to help the Africans prepare their case. When we saw what he had done, we thought that Priscus could not go before the judges. He had behaved in such a cruel and inhuman way. We felt he would have to stand trial because he had accepted bribes to condemn people who were innocent. He had even put people to death for money.

Fronto Catius defended Priscus. He said there should be no trial. He wanted the Senate just to get the money back. Catius is very good at winning people to his side. He can make them feel so sorry for someone that they weep for them. He put on every scrap of canvas that day to steer his ship away from a trial.

So an almighty row broke out and the Senate was split into two factions. Some said the law was quite clear. Because Priscus had pleaded guilty, he could not be put on trial. Others said the matter was still open and we could say what we liked. They also said that when Priscus was put on trial, he should be punished for whatever he said he had done. Iulius Ferox, who was **Consul-elect**, is a good and blessed man. He said that Priscus should be sent before the judges, but all those who had been named for bribing Priscus to kill innocent people, should be called as witnesses.

All the Senators agreed with this view. In fact there was so much bitter quarrelling that this was the only view they would talk about. You know how it goes. When someone in the Senate speaks strongly for something and arouses the pity of the Senators, this is the view which sparks into life and catches fire. But when you take good advice and think about it carefully, the flames are put out and the fires die away. When everyone is shouting around, many Senators are ready to support something which they would not speak for on their own. Talking in a crowd only fogs the issue. It is only when you get away from the crowd, you get away from the fog. You can then see properly what should be done.

The Senate called two witnesses from Africa, Vitellius Honoratus and Flavius Marcianus. Honoratus was charged with bribing Priscus with 300,000 sesterces. Priscus took the money and sent a Roman Knight into exile. He also put to death seven of the Knight's friends. Marcianus was charged with giving Priscus 700,000 sesterces. For this money Priscus had inflicted many different punishments on another Roman Knight. The poor man had been beaten up with clubs, and condemned to the mines. Then he was sent to prison, where he was strangled.

Honoratus was lucky. He didn't come before the Senate because he died. When Marcianus was brought in to the Senate, Priscus was not there. And so, Tuccius Cerialis, who was a **Consular**, used the right to speak, which every Senator has. He said that Priscus should be told that Marcianus was up before the Senate.

I do not know why he did this. He may have thought Priscus would get more sympathy or be hated more, if he were there. Or possibly it is fairest that a charge which involves two people, should be defended by both of them together. If the charge is proved, then both should be punished. I think this is why Tuccius said Priscus should be there.

Well, the whole business was postponed until the next meeting of the Senate and this was a most blessed occasion. The Princeps presided over the Senate. He did this because he was Consul. It was now the month of January, when the city was crowded out with people, especially Senators. Not only that. The trial was such an important one. When it was postponed, it was given even greater publicity. There is also something about human nature. No-one can help being curious about something important and unusual.

Try and conjure up how panic-stricken we were! We had to make a speech on a matter so important in such an important place, under the very eyes of Caesar. I had made speeches in the Senate before and the Senate had always listened very kindly to what I said. But this was all new and I was chilled to the bone with fear. These were all the problems I have just mentioned but there was something else which was difficult to deal with.

The man on trial in the Senate had been Consul and an important state priest. Both these honours had now been taken away from him. Because he had behaved so cruelly, it was clear his cruelty would go against him. Because he had been stripped of these honours, it was clear Senators would have sympathy for him. It was a very serious thing to attack a man who had just been condemned like this.

Well, I pulled myself and my thoughts together. When I made my speech, the Senators met my fear with their sympathy. I spoke for almost five hours. They let me have twelve full water-clocks and another four as well. You know when you are about to make a speech, the sea seems stormy and set against you. But when you are actually speaking, it is all fair weather and plain sailing.

Indeed Caesar showed his great concern and care for me. (It would be wrong to use the word 'anxiety'.) Time and time again he told the freedman who was standing behind me that I should be careful with my voice and lungs. I am rather delicate by nature and he thought I was trying too hard. Claudius Marcellinus defended Priscus and spoke against me. When he had spoken, the meeting was then adjourned until the next day. It could not have gone on much longer anyway because it was getting dark.

On the next day Salvius Liberalis defended Priscus. Salvius is very good with words. He sets out what he has to say very carefully. He is sharp and hits hard. He can speak really well. On that day he did his very best. Cornelius Tacitus spoke against him most eloquently. He also spoke with great dignity. When you think of Tacitus, dignity is what you think about. Fronto Catius then spoke up for Priscus. He did this very well but he spent more time asking for mercy for Priscus than defending him. At this stage in the trial this was the sort of move you expect him to make. Fronto finished his speech just as it was getting dark. So the closing speeches were put off until the third day. For a meeting of the Senate to be adjourned at night, and then resumed and finished on the third day was a fine old-fashioned thing to do.

Cornutus Tertullus made three proposals. Priscus should be made to pay back to the Treasury the 700,000 sesterces he had taken. He should be exiled from the city and Italy. Marcianus should be exiled from the city, Italy and Africa. Cornutus was Consul-elect and a very good man. He fights hard for the truth. At the end of his speech he added that the Senate thought we had done well. He felt that I and Tacitus had worked hard and spoken up with courage. The other Consuls-elect agreed with Cornutus, as did all the other Consulars until it was the turn of Pompeius Collega to speak. He said Priscus should pay back the 700,000 to the Treasury and

Marcianus should be exiled for 5 years. But as Priscus had already been punished for taking bribes by losing his rank and his priesthood, he felt that was enough.

The Senate did not know what to do. Many Senators liked the suggestion of Cornutus. Perhaps even more liked the idea of Collega. What Collega wanted was not as hard on Priscus. Some Senators first of all liked what Cornutus said but after they heard Collega speak, they agreed with him. But when the Senators had to vote, something very interesting happened.

Those who stood next to the Consuls [and the Emperor was a Consul] went and stood with Cornutus. Then those who would have been counted as supporters of Collega, crossed the floor and stood with Cornutus. In the end Collega was left almost on his own. Collega later complained bitterly about his 'friends' who had set him up. He was very angry with Regulus who had told him word for word what to say and then deserted him. Regulus is always changing his mind. He is fickle. He always bites off more than he can chew and then he gets cold feet!

This was how that splendid trial finished. There is only one small matter left to deal with. Hostilius Firminus, the assistant to Marius Priscus was mixed up with the bribery. This is clear from the accounts which Marcianus showed which Firminus made to the local Senate at Lepcis. Firminus had used his own talent to help Priscus in his evil plans. He has now seen his own career fall in ruins because of this.

Firminus was found guilty of trying to obtain 200,000 sesterces from Marcianus and of receiving 10,000 sesterces. This was put down in his accounts under 'for his perfumer'. This fits him very well because he is such a big pansy. Cornutus proposed that his case should be heard at the next meeting of the Senate and we agreed.

Firminus was not at this meeting of the Senate. He may have been away by chance or he may have had a bad conscience.

There you are. You have all the city news. Fill me in on what is going on in the country. How are your fruit trees, your vines, your cows and those 'prize' sheep? And if you don't send me back a letter as long as this, all you'll get from me in the future is a very very short note!

(II.11)

26. Kilroy was here

To Maesius Maximus

We used to vote in the Senate by putting our hands in the air and being counted. Now no-one can see how we vote because we use voting **tablets**. I was afraid some people would take advantage of them and they have. In the recent elections some people scribbled on the tablets. Some of it was funny, some of it was filthy. On one tablet where the names of the candidates should have been filled in, they put the names of the people who proposed them.

When the senators heard about it, they glowed white hot with anger. They demanded the Princeps should bring down his anger on the person who had done it. But the person who had done it, did not own up. And he didn't give himself away. He may even have been in the crowd of those who shouted for the culprit to be punished.

Think of this man. On such a serious occasion he messes about. He thinks the Senate is the place to show how slick and smart he is. What must he be like at home? This secret way of voting lets the wicked do what they want to do. Think of him again. He comes up and demands a voting tablet. He is given something to write with; he puts his head down and writes. He doesn't give a damn for anyone, not even himself. He writes what you can see on the walls of lavatories.

What can you do? How can you find a cure for this? The distaste is much too strong for us. We are lazy, rash and selfish. That means He has to work all the harder to help us.

(IV.25)

27. A problem for the Senate

To Iulius Valerianus

Here is something for you to think about. It is only a little thing but it may grow into something much bigger. Sollers, a man who had been praetor, asked the Senate to let him hold a market once a week on his own land. The people of Vicetia did not want this to happen. They asked Tuscilius Nominatus to speak for them in the Senate against Sollers.

The Senate put the case off until another meeting. Then

the people of Vicetia came without anyone to speak for them. They said they had been cheated. They had either foolishly trusted what Nominatus had said or they felt they had been cheated but may not have been.

They were asked by the praetor whom had they asked to speak for them. They said Nominatus. When asked if he was going to do this for nothing, they said they had first of all given him 6,000 sesterces. They had then given him 4,000 more. The praetor asked the Senate to make Nominatus appear.

That is what has happened so far. But we will hear more of this. Many points have only been touched upon. The dust, once stirred, will rise.

I hope I have made you prick up your ears. You will have to be very kind to me for a long time to come if you want to hear the end of the story. Unless, of course, you come to Rome to see for yourself!

(V.4)

28. Informers, Emperors and Games

To Sempronius Rufus

Our most noble Princeps asked me to be a member of his **Council**, to sort out a problem. The people of Vienna are going to put on some Games. They have been left the money to do so. But Trebonius Rufus, a good man and a friend of mine, has seen to it that they are stopped and not put on again. Trebonius is one of the **duumviri**.

The people of Vienna say he does not have the authority to do this. He says he has. When they came before the Senate, Trebonius spoke well enough to win. And win he did. He was serious and he made sense. This went down well, especially when we knew he felt very strongly about this.

Other Senators said what they thought. Iunius Mauricus said the people of Vienna must not get the Games back ever. You will not find a man who is more brave or more true than he. He also said, 'I wish they could be stopped at Rome.' You may think that was a brave and noble thing to say. If you do, then you don't know Mauricus. He did the same thing to the Emperor Nerva.

Nerva once had a few close friends in for dinner. One, Veiento, was next to him and lay almost in his lap. When I mention Veiento by name and tell you he was an informer, you'll know all about him. During the dinner they got talking about Catullus Messalinus, another informer. As you know, Catullus had lost the sight of both eyes but this had made him all the more vicious. He was afraid of no-one. He had no sense of shame. He did not pity anyone. The Emperor Domitian used him like a spear, blind and unfeeling, to kill anyone who was any good.

Anyway, Nerva and his friends were talking about how evil Catullus was, when the Emperor Nerva himself asked, 'What do you think would happen to him if he were alive today?' Mauricus said, 'He would be having dinner with us.'

Well, to get back to the Games at Vienna, we decided to stop them. They had got such a hold on the people. So have the games in Rome. What goes on in Vienna, only affects Vienna. What happens here affects everyone everywhere. Our empire is like a body. If something affects the head, it also affects all the parts.

(IV.22)

C · Pliny as a businessman

All the letters in this section are about farming and running estates. This is because Pliny was a big landowner. This is where he made most of his money.

Pliny owned land in three parts of Italy: (1) He owned four villas near the city of Rome. Each villa had its own estate. The villas at Tusculum, Praeneste and Tibur were just country houses where he could work and relax. His villa and estate at Laurentum had woods, fields for sheep, horses and cattle and produced good milk. It was as much a farm as a country house. As a farm it might earn Pliny some money. The other villas would earn him nothing. (2) Pliny also had an estate 150 miles north of Rome at Tifernum Tiberinum. He rented this estate out to tenants and got 400,000 sesterces a year in rent. The estate was by the river and in winter and spring Pliny sent what it produced by boat to Rome. This was usually corn and wine. (3) Pliny also owned several villas in the north of Italy. These were near Comum where he was born. Two of the villas were built over Lake Como.

We would call Pliny a very wealthy man. He may have owned more than ten villas. Each villa would be huge when compared to our three bedroom semi-detached house. Most of the villas had a large estate with them. It would be hard to run these estates properly. Pliny had all the problems that farmers always have — bad harvests and tenant farmers who cannot pay the rent.

Also because Pliny was so busy in Rome, he could only visit his land rarely. When Pliny visited Comum in A.D. 104 we know he had not been there for over eight years. When Pliny goes to his estates, he writes about them in an odd way. He seems to look down on country problems. They are a bore and bring him no pleasure. He is bothered about what goes wrong and not what goes right. He seems to be uneasy about being in the country. He does not seem to get involved. The

only way he can get round his uneasiness is to do what he
does in the city, write.

But this is only the picture Pliny wanted to give his friends.
The truth may be very different. We know Pliny runs ten or
more houses, estates in three parts of Italy, with slaves, tenants, and crops which he sells. He writes books, speeches,
poems and is a full-time politician in Rome. He also buys land
and manages the estates of his close relatives. To do all that
he must have been very well organised. He may also have been
interested in and very good at running his estates.

29. Farms, profits and writing

To Julius Naso
A storm of hail has ruined my grapes in Etruria. My farm
beyond the River Po has produced a bumper crop but they
tell me the market price is poor. I have only got my farm at
Laurentum to bring me in any profit. Even so I do not have
anything there worth any real money. There is only the farm
building, the garden and the beach which comes up to it.

Still it does bring me in a profit and I cannot say that of
my other farms. You see, I do most of my writing at my farm
at Laurentum. I do not cultivate fields that I do not have but
I write. And by writing I cultivate myself!

From my other farms I could show you granaries full of
crops. Here I can show you a desk full of what I have written.
So if you want to be like me and have set your heart on a
farm which will bring you a profit, find yourself a little place
on this part of the coast.

(IV.6)

30. To buy or not to buy

To Calvisius Rufus
Can I do what I always do? I want to ask your advice on
something which is to do with my 'familia'. There is an estate
next to mine which is up for sale. There are many reasons
why I want to buy it and also many reasons why I do not.

It would be nice to join up both estates. This is what

attracts me and makes me want to buy it. Not only would it look good, it would also be a useful thing to do. I could go round both estates on one and the same visit. I could use the same farm manager and the same foremen to run both estates. I would only have to keep one house open. The other one I need only keep in good repair. I am also thinking about the cost of furniture, slaves to run the house, gardeners, workmen, and even the cost of equipment for hunting. As far as expense goes, there is a big difference between keeping all these in one place and having them in many different places.

But I am afraid of storms and other disasters. So I do not want to put all my eggs in one basket. It seems safer to have estates in many different places. That is the way to soften the blows of Fortune. And when you have to travel to different places, the change does you good. When you have to visit your different estates, that is pleasant too. All these are important details but the real reason I want to buy it is this. The land is fertile, rich and well watered. The estate is made up of fields, vineyards and woods which provide timber and some sort of profit, even if it is only a small one.

However the tenants who farm the land are stupid. They have let all the goodness drain away from the land. The last owner made the tenants sell their possessions to pay what they owed him. He got rid of their debts sure enough. But by selling all they had, he made them unable to pay anything in the future. Now the tenants are exhausted and getting into debt again. If I buy the estate now, I shall have to equip it with slaves bought specially for the job. This will push the cost up, because the slaves must be free to work. As you know, I do not have any gangs of slaves kept in chains on my farms. No-one does there either.

All you need to know is how much they want for it. 3 million sesterces. They wanted 5 million but the price has gone down because it is so difficult to find tenants for the farms. Times are hard anyway. Can I easily find the 3 million? I have nearly all my money invested in land, apart from a small amount which I loan to others. But I can always borrow it. My mother-in-law will let me have it. She lets me use her money as if it were mine. So if you are happy about the other points I mention, you can forget about this one.

Please consider the matter very carefully. You have a great

deal of experience of making the most of what you have got. You also always know what to do for the best in the long term.

(III.19)

31. Trying to work in the country

To Falco
You will find this difficult to believe but I had to run away to Etruria to do what I had to do. Yet I find it cannot be done! I am being worn out by letters and complaints from my tenants all around me. You can tell how I feel when I say I like reading their stuff less than I like reading my own. (And you know how little I like reading that.) I am trying to look at some of my own little efforts again. I have left it too long and it has become a slow and deadly business. I had also hoped to do the accounts of the estate, now that I am here. But I might as well not be here, for all the work I have done on them.

Still sometimes I jump on a horse and ride round part of my estate, playing out the part of being the owner. At least the exercise does me good. Can I ask you to do as you always do? Keep sending long letters full of city life to me buried here in the country.

(IX.15)

32. New wine and new poems

To Mamilianus
You write to say that you could not even begin to count what you have caught. That is just what some writers of history say. If you caught that many when you were hunting, I am not surprised you enjoyed it so much. I have not got the time for hunting, because we are busy picking the grape harvest. Also I do not feel like it because there is not much to pick. I shall not be able to send this year's wine along to you. I will let you have this year's new poems instead. I

know how much pleasure it will give you to taste these. I
shall send them to you just as soon as they have fermented.

(IX.16)

33. Books and grapes

To Venator
I was pleased with your letter because it was a long one. I was
particularly pleased too because all you talked about was my
little books. I am not surprised that they give you pleasure. I
know you love all my books just as much as you love me.

I am now busy gathering in the grape harvest which is light.
Even so it is richer than I expected. But I am not sure that
you could call what I do 'gathering in'. I pick the odd grape.
I pop in and look at the wine press. I taste the new wine fer-
menting in the vat and creep up on the slaves which I have
brought from the city with me. They are now in charge of
the farm workers and leave me to my secretaries and readers.

(IX.20)

34. Rents and debts

To Valerius Paulinus
There are some things that friends usually do for friends. But
you are not the sort of person who insists that your close
friends should do these, when they have a problem. My problem is this.

I cannot be present in the Senate when you become Consul.
Because I love you so much, I am sure that you will fully
understand why. I am about to let out my farms on long
leases and I have to stop here to see that it is done properly. I
have also got to find a better way of doing it.

In the past I have let the farms on five-year leases. During
that time I have also had to reduce the rents. But even so my
tenants have not been able to pay the rent. They have got
more and more into debt. They are now so behind in their
payments that they will never be able to pay off all they owe.
So now most of them do not even care about paying up at all.
They are just like pirates plundering the land. They do not see

how their lives and the land are connected. They do not realise that when they neglect the crops, they neglect themselves. This is silly but it is happening more and more.

This is a problem which I have to solve. There is only one way out. I must stop letting out the farms for a fixed sum of money. Instead I must take a fixed amount of what they produce as rent. I could also put some of my own slaves in the farms. These could get my share of the produce for me and keep an eye on the harvest.

The rewards you get from working hard on the land are the best in all the world. But to get them you need to have great faith, keen eyes and plenty of help. Still I must do something. I feel like a doctor treating an illness that will not go away. I shall have to try everything I can to bring about a change for the better.

So it is business, not pleasure that stops me coming to see you made Consul. On that day I shall pray for you. I shall rejoice with you. I shall congratulate you. I shall do that here in Tuscany just as much as if I were with you in Rome.

(IX.37)

35. Pliny's villa at Laurentum

The villa is big enough for all my needs and it does not cost too much to keep in order. As you go in, you see the **atrium**[1] which is plain but not mean. Beyond it are two colonnades which form the shape of a letter D. They enclose a courtyard[2] which is quite small but attractive. This is a splendid place when the weather is really bad, because it is protected by windows and its overhanging roof.

Beyond this is a very pleasant inner court[3] and then a dining room[4] which is delightful enough. This room runs out onto the seashore, and when the sea is driven inshore by the southwest wind, the tiny ripples from the breakers just lightly wash up against it. It has folding doors and windows which are the same size as the doors. From the front and the sides the room seems to face three different seas. The back of this dining room has a very different view. From it you look right through the house into the inner courtyard, the D-shaped courtyard with its two colonnades, and onto the atrium and out to the woods and far distant mountains.

To the left of this and slightly farther back is a large bed-room[5] and next to this another smaller one.[6] There are two windows in this bedroom, one of which lets in the early morning sunshine, the other one holds on to the rays of the setting sun. From here you can see the sea more safely although it is farther away. There is a corner where the walls of the large bedroom and the dining room meet, which is a perfect suntrap. This corner[7] catches the sun's rays and magnifies them. My household use this corner for the winter quarters and for their gymnasium. The only winds which can disturb the peace of that place are those which bring the heavy storms, and even while they are doing their worst, the corner is never put out of action.

Next to this corner is a room[8] which is curved in the shape of an apse. As the sun goes round during the day, it always shines through some of the windows of this room. One wall is fitted out with shelves and looks like a library. On these shelves I keep the books which I love to read again and again, rather than the well-known classics. Next to this is a bedroom[9] with a floor which is raised on piles and fitted out with central heating. The pipes in the central heating distribute the steam and see that it heats the place to the right temperature. The rest of this side of the house[10] is given up to the needs of the slaves and freedmen. Even so most of the rooms are quite good enough for guests to stay in.

On the other side of the dining room, there is a really elegant bedroom[11] and next to it a room which can be used either as a large bedroom or a modest dining room.[12] This room is full of sun and sea. Behind it is another room with an antechamber.[13] Because it is sheltered from all the winds, it is cool in summer and warm in winter.

There is also a second room, with its own antechamber, joined to the first by a single wall. Next to it is the cooling room of the baths[14] which is on the big side and rather spread out. Two small baths face each other from opposite walls. The baths themselves are quite big enough when you consider how close the sea is. Then comes the oiling room,[15] the sweating room[16] and the boiler house.[17] Close to them is a marvellous heated swimming pool[18] from which swimmers can see the sea.

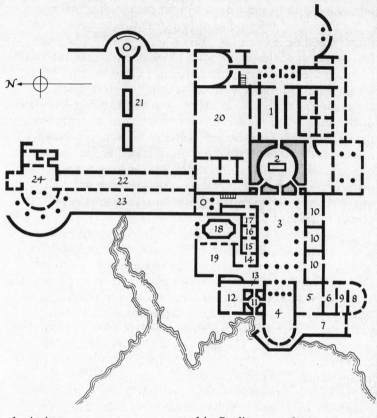

1. Atrium
2. Courtyard
3. Inner courtyard
4. Dining room
5. Bedroom
6. Bedroom
7. Gymnasium
8. Bedroom
9. Bedroom
10. Slaves' room
11. Bedroom
12. Small dining room
13. Rooms and antechambers
14. Cooling room for baths
15. Oiling room for baths
16. Sweating room for baths
17. Boiler house for baths
18. Heated swimming-bath
19. Ball court
20. Kitchen garden
21. Ornamental garden with vine pergola
22. Covered arcade
23. Terrace
24. Pliny's private suite

Figure 1. Pliny's villa at Laurentum

Figure 2. A model of Pliny's villa.

Pliny goes on to mention other features of the house which included a ball court,[19] a kitchen,[20] an ornamental garden,[21] and a covered arcade[22] with a fine terrace[23] in front of it. At the end of this was a suite of rooms[24] which Pliny built for himself and which he really loved. Here he had a study, a restroom and two bedrooms. It was here that he would come either to work or to get away from the noise of his slaves celebrating the **Saturnalia** in the main part of the house.

(II.17)

36. Spending a day in the country

To Fuscus
You want to know how I spend the days in summer on my farm in Etruria. I wake up when I like, usually about dawn, often earlier (hardly ever later). I keep the shutters on the windows closed. When it is quiet and dark, I do not have anything to distract me. I am left all to myself. When you are out in the daylight, your eyes control your mind and tell it what to think about. When you are in the dark, it is the other way round. Your eyes see what your mind sees.

If I am in the middle of writing something, I think about that. I think about putting in this word or altering that one. Sometimes I can do quite a lot of this. At other times I do not get very far. It depends on how easy or how difficult it is to put things together and remember them.

After that I call in a secretary, have the shutters opened and let in the day. Then I dictate to him what I have made up in my bed. He goes away. I call him back then I send him off again. I do not do things by the clock but at ten or eleven — it depends on what sort of day it is — I go off to the terrace or the covered gallery. Here I think out the rest of what I am working on and dictate it to a secretary. Then I go for a drive. On the drive I do the same thing as I do when I am out for a walk or lying down. I write. If I keep changing what I do, I find I can keep on writing. After that I have a nap and then go for a walk. And before I know where I am, I am reading a speech in Greek or in Latin. I try to do this clearly and with proper expression. I want not only to improve my voice but also my digestion. Reading aloud properly makes your voice and your digestion strong.

After I have had another walk, my slaves anoint me with oil, put me through my exercises and give me a bath. At dinner, with my wife or a few friends, I have a slave read me a book. After dinner I listen to a slave reading a comedy or another slave playing the lyre. Then I am off out again walking with my 'familia', some of whom are well educated. We have all sorts of discussions which keep us awake far into the night. But however long the day is, it is always nicely put to bed.

Of course, I do not do the same thing day in and day out. Supposing I have spent a long time lying down or on my walk — well then, after my nap and time for reading I go for a ride on one of my horses rather than use my carriage. It is quicker and saves me time. Sometimes friends who live near, break in on me and steal a part of my day. If they break in on me when I am tired, they do me a favour.

Now and then I go hunting but I always take my tablets with me to write on. So even if I catch nothing, I still bring something back home with me. I also give some time to the tenants on my farms. They never think it is enough. Their country grumbles only make our writings and our great deeds in the city well worth doing.

(IX.36)

D · Pliny as a writer

Pliny saw himself as a great writer. Writing was one of the things he liked to do best. He wrote:

1. Poems. These included a tragedy written in Greek when he was 14. Throughout his life he also wrote Latin poems in various metres.
2. Legal speeches. They were often about wills and inheritances. He wrote these for when he appeared as a lawyer in the Centumviral Court.
3. Great public speeches. He prosecuted three ex-governors of Roman provinces and defended two others. He also thanked the Emperor Trajan for being so good. He had to write speeches for all this. He spoke these in the Senate.
4. Local speeches. He wrote a speech which he read out when he opened a library at Comum.
5. Letters to friends. We have ten books of his letters. Books I to IX were written to friends. Book X contains letters to the Emperor Trajan, together with his replies.

Not only was he a writer he was also a great publisher. Writing a speech and having it published are not the same thing. Pliny because he was a lawyer and an orator, did read out aloud much of what he had written. He also revised what he wrote, he altered words, he changed parts and he added more. He would then publish this new version. This is why the letters are rather odd. What we now have are carefully revised versions of letters which he actually wrote. They are not like ordinary everyday letters but more like specially written essays. This is odd in a real letter. Pliny's everyday letters have been turned by him into a book of good manners. They are meant to show how a man of sense and good taste should behave.

There are three other things which are important about Pliny's letters. Many Romans believed that the way to cheat death was to be written about. A Roman wrote a speech about his father-in-law in which he said, 'People will forget so many of those who are now dead. They will lie dead without fame or glory but my father-in-law will be alive for ever. This is because he has been written about. He now belongs to those who will be born.' A Roman poet said that the poems he had written would last longer than the pyramids. Pliny certainly believes in this as an idea. He often says in the letters that writing is the way to make sure you live on after death.

Pliny is also very much concerned with what people will think of him while he is alive. He wants fame both in death and in life. He wants to have his cake and eat it. This is why nine out of the ten books of letters were published in his lifetime. When these were published, he became something of a star, a personality, a celebrity. The letters proclaim what a man Pliny was. They show how he thought he behaved in his private life. They showed what Pliny had done in his public life. In many ways Pliny, like most men, was like Narcissus. Narcissus was the boy who looked into the pool of water and fell in love with his own reflection. He keeps on and on thinking about himself. The letters of Pliny are about Pliny far more than they are about anything else.

In many ways Pliny is a clever man. He is crafty. He is not very honest and often very irritating. He always has to win. If you look again at letter 10 you can see this. In this letter Pliny's grandfather-in-law thinks Pliny has done wrong. The last thing Pliny will do is admit this.

Although Pliny is clever, he is not clever enough. Because he was so busy thinking about what others thought of him in this world, he did not become a first-rate artist. What he says is certainly interesting. He gives us valuable evidence for how some Romans lived. But the real weakness of his letters is that they are not private enough.

37. Be a writer and cheat death

To Caninius Rufus

How is our darling Comum getting on? How is that pleasant little house, just outside the town? And what about the colonnade, where it is always spring? And the plane tree that is so shady? How is the stream, all green and sparkling? And the lake below it that is its slave? What about the drives with their soft firm grass, the baths which the sun fills and visits every day, the dining rooms, large and small, and the rooms for rest and sleep?

Have they got their hold on you? Do they make you visit each of them every day, or are you for ever being called away to sort out some family business? You are lucky and blessed, if they have got you in their power. If they have not, you are just like everyone else. Why don't you hand over those miserable cares that you love to someone else? It's about time that you did. You ought to hide yourself away in that high rich study of yours and do some real work with the books. That would be both business and pleasure, work and rest. You should put all your energies into that day and night.

Become an artist! Shape out something that will be you forever. When you are dead, everything you own will be given to another master. That is the way that Fortune works. But what you write, will always belong to you, if only you make a start.

I think I know you very well. You have plenty of spirit and real talent. You must work hard to be the great man you will be. When you are great, others then will see you for what you will be.

(I.3)

38. Poems in Greek and Latin

To Arrius Antoninus
You have written some epigrams in Greek and I have been trying to put them into Latin. Here am I trying to do as well as you. See how much I admire you! But it's no good. My poems are not as good as yours. I have no talent and as the Latin poet Lucretius says, 'Latin is a poor language for poetry.' You may feel that these poems in Latin, and done by me, are charming. Try and imagine how lovely are those written by you in Greek.

(IV.18)

39. Why Pliny invites friends to hear him read a speech

To Terentius Scaurus

I was going to give a reading of a little speech which I am thinking about publishing. So I invited some friends to hear me, just enough to make me feel afraid, but not too many to stop me hearing the truth. I always have two reasons for giving a reading. First of all, I want to be made nervous. When I am nervous, I am always more careful in what I try to do. Secondly the friends who come, often correct for me those mistakes which are mine and no-one else's.

This is just what happened in this case. I was lucky enough to find friends who were very helpful. I also myself made a note of some things that will have to be altered. I have now made the alterations and I am sending the speech to you. You will know what it is about from the title. As for anything else, the book itself will make it clear. You will be able to understand it, without any introduction.

Please write and let me know what you think of the speech as a whole. Let me know as well what you think of the parts of it. I need to know your opinion before I decide not to have it published or before I go ahead and let it out.

(V.12)

40. Write something

To Geminus

I was very pleased to have your letter, especially because you want me to write something to put in one of your books. I will think of something to write about. I may do what you suggest but I am not too happy about it. If you think hard about what you have suggested, you will see why. So I may do something else.

I didn't think there were any bookshops at Lugdunum. So I was all the more pleased when you said my books were on sale there. I am happy that they sell as well out there as they do in the city. What I write must be really worth something when people who live so far away from each other think they are good.

(IX.11)

41. Reading poems aloud

To Tranquillus

I am caught in a cold sweat and I want you to help me out. I hear that I do not read poetry well. I can read speeches out well enough but that makes my reading of poetry aloud all the worse. I am going to invite some close friends here and I am planning to have read to them something I have written, I might get one of my freedmen to do it. Then I will keep it within the 'familia'. I have a freedman in mind. I have chosen him not because he can read well, but because he can read better than I can, if he is not nervous. He is new to reading to an audience as I am new to writing poetry.

I do not know what I shall do when he is reading what I have written. I could sit still, with my eyes fixed, not saying a word. I could pretend to be someone who has come to hear someone else's poem and not the person who wrote it. Or I could do what others do, when they hear what they have written being read for them. They mouth the words. They flash their eyes. They use their hands. In fact the only thing they do not do is speak! But my mouthings, flashings and gestures are as bad as my reading aloud!

So come on! Help me out of this sweat I am in. Write back and tell me the truth. Is it better for me to read badly than do or not do those things?

(IX.34)

E · Bithynia

Pliny was sent out by the Emperor Trajan as governor of the province of Bithynia with Pontus in about A.D. 110. He went out with a grandiose and impressive title — *'Legatus Augusti pro praetore consular potestate'*. He was officially 'Imperial praetorian governor with the full power of the Consuls'. This meant when he went about his business in the province he had an escort of twelve lictors — each one carrying the fasces. These were sets of rods with axes in them, symbolising the power of Rome. He also had a deputy and small administrative staff. He did not have very many troops under his command.

Trajan had sent him out there for two reasons. First of all, he was worried about the way the cities of the province had been spending money. Some cities had spent money on things which were forbidden by law. Others had spent public money very badly and corruption was suspected. Private citizens had also somehow got their hands on and spent public monies for their own benefit. Secondly, Trajan was worried about law and order. He did not want to see the peace of the province disturbed. In particular he wanted to keep a careful eye on local politics to stop any illegal political organisations springing up. This is why Pliny looked very carefully at the Christians.

Once again when we look at Pliny's letters we have to be careful when we come to judge them. The letters presented here are only part of the whole correspondence between Pliny and Trajan. Some people when they read all the letters feel that Pliny could not decide anything for himself and had to consult the Emperor the whole of the time. This is not true. Pliny wrote only 61 letters to Trajan in some two years. Of these only 40 were enquiries, which the Emperor had authorised Pliny to write about in cases of doubt. Only twice did Trajan feel that Pliny should not have bothered him. It is quite clear too that Pliny got on with his work and took many of his own decisions without referring to the Emperor. If quick action was needed he couldn't wait for a reply all the way from Rome, anyway. It is also interesting to see how careful Pliny is when he writes to Trajan. Pliny is always aware that Trajan is far above him. Pliny knows too that it was what the Emperor wanted that mattered most. The Emperor Domitian loved to feel better than anyone else. He liked being called **'Dominus et Deus'** — 'Master and Lord God'. Although no-one called Trajan **'Deus'** — 'Lord God', Pliny calls him **'Dominus'** — 'Master'. There are times too when Pliny uses religious words to talk about the Emperor and speaks of him as if he were a god. If you look back at the last paragraph of letter 26, you can see something of this. There are signs of this in this last section of letters.

Trajan's replies are interesting. Some scholars feel that they were written by the civil service back in Rome and that the Emperor had very little to do with them. Others think Trajan wrote them all.

The first letter is not from Pliny's correspondence with Trajan. It is Pliny's own advice to a friend who has just been

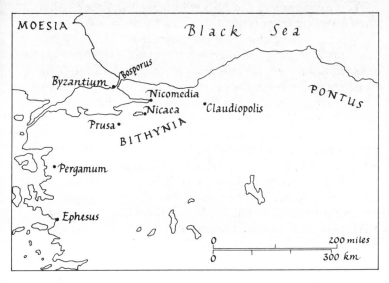

Map 3. Bithynia and Pontus

appointed governor of Greece. You might compare what Pliny says a governor should do with what he actually did himself.

42. Pliny gives advice to a man who is going to govern Achaia

To Maximus

My love for you forces me not to give you instructions. You do not need anyone to do that. But it makes me want to give you a warning. Be true to what you know. If you are not, then know nothing!

Just think where you are going. You have been sent to the province of Achaia. Achaia is the true and only Greece. Achaia is the place where humanity, literature and even our daily bread was first discovered.

You have been sent out to bring good government and order to those cities which are free, to men who are men, to the free who are free. You are going to men who obey the law because they are born to do so. They have kept the law by being brave and by doing great deeds. They have held on to it by winning friends, by making contacts with others and by worshipping the gods.

You must respect the gods who make the Greeks what they are. You must respect the very names of their gods. Respect too their glory and their age. If we honour a man who has lived long, we must worship a city which is old. You must honour them because they are old, because they have done great deeds, and because they have such fine legends. Do not steal from anyone their dignity or their freedom. And if they want to boast, let them!

Always remember that Achaia is the land which gave us the laws. They did not impose the law on us, because they had defeated us in battle. No. When we came and asked them for laws, they freely gave them to us. It is to Athens that you are going. It is Sparta that you are ruling. Only a complete savage could rip from them what is left of their freedom and good name. Often slaves and masters are ill with the same disease. The doctors are always much kinder to those who are not slaves.

You must remember how each city was. When you do

remember, do not look down upon it, because it is no longer great. Do not be proud. Do not be rough. Be gentle and kind. They will not look down on you for this. No-one who comes with the power and majesty of Rome is looked down upon unless he turns out to be mean and common. The first person such a man looks down upon is himself. You must not force people to do things they should not do, just to build up your own power. You must not try to win respect by terrorising them. If they love you, they will do what you want far more willingly than if they fear you. Fear flies away when you go, but love stays behind forever. Fear turns into hatred; love turns into respect.

I must say this again. You have been sent out 'to bring good government and order to the free cities'. You must think carefully what this means and how big a job it is. What could be better than good order and peace? What could be worse than the breakdown of good order and the death of freedom?

But you must be careful. You were popular when you were a quaestor in Bithynia. You came back to Rome with a fine reputation. It is this which is now weighing you down. Other things do weigh you down — the backing of the Princeps, your successful career in politics and this present job which was given to you as a reward for all your efforts. In many ways you are your own worst enemy. It was easier to do better in a province at the ends of the earth. It will be more difficult to do so in a province near Rome. It was easier to work among free men. It will be harder to work among slaves. It was easier when you had a post given you by lot. It will be harder now you have been specially chosen by the Emperor. It was easier when you were young and inexperienced. It will be harder now you have experience and are successful. If you do not have a reputation, you cannot lose one. But it is a great disgrace to lose a reputation if you have got one.

As I said at the beginning of this letter, I am giving you a warning, rather than instructing you. But I am, of course, giving you instructions as well. When I love someone, I do not see why I should tie myself down. You cannot say too much, when you ought to say as much as possible.

(VIII.24)

43. Problems in getting to Bithynia

To Trajan, the Emperor
Master, everything went very well on the voyage, until I got
to Ephesus. When I got there, I began to travel by carriage
but I was troubled with the heat, which was very bad. I also
went down with a slight fever. So I had to stop at Pergamum.

I then got on one of the ships that go round the coast but
I was held back by winds blowing in the other direction. In
the end I entered Bithynia on September 17th. This was a
little later than I had expected. I cannot, however, complain
of the delay because I was really lucky. I arrived in the province just at the right moment to celebrate your birthday.

I am now shaking out the expenses, the income and the
debts of the city of Prusa. The busier I am the more I see how
necessary it is. Private citizens have been hanging on to large
sums of money for all sorts of reasons. Other big sums of
money have been paid out by the city quite wrongly.

I have just got here, master, and here am I writing to you.

(X.17a)

44. Pliny asks for a surveyor

To Trajan, the Emperor
I entered the province, Master, on September 17th. I found
here the same good feeling towards you and the same love for
you that you deserve from all mankind.

Look and see, Master, whether you ought to send a sur-
veyor here. A lot of money can be got back from the building
contractors, if the surveys are done honestly. This is certainly
true of the accounts at Prusa. I am looking at these with great
care.

(X.17b)

45. Trajan tells Pliny why he has been sent to Bithynia

To Pliny
I wish that you could have got to Bithynia without the
slightest harm to your poor self or your people. I also wish
that your journey from Ephesus had been as easy as your

voyage there. I know, my dearest Pliny, from your letter the day on which you reached Bithynia. Those who live in that province will know that I am looking after them. You must also put yourself out to show them that I have chosen you to stand for me. The first thing you must do is this. You must 'shake out' the accounts of the cities. Everyone knows they are in a mess.

I do not have enough surveyors for the building that has to be done in and around Rome. There are surveyors who can be trusted. You will find them in every province. All you have to do is to work hard and 'shake them out' too!

(X.18)

46. Slaves, soldiers and prisons

To Trajan
Master, I do not know what to do. So I ask you to give me some direction. Should I let public slaves be prison officers? This is what they have done up to now. Or should I use Roman soldiers for this? Public slaves do not make the best prison officers. But you would need a fair number of soldiers to do the job.

For the time being, I have added a few soldiers to the slaves. There is a danger that neither the soldiers nor the slaves will do the job properly. If they both do it, they may have enough cheek to blame each other.

(X.19)

47. Trajan tells Pliny what to do

To Pliny
My dearest Pliny, there is no need for more of my soldiers to be used to guard the prisoners. Let the public slaves do this. That is what has been done in the past in the province. And that is what we must do now.

It is your job to see that they do this properly. You will need to be quite strict over this. As you say in your letter, we must be very careful when we mix Roman soldiers in with public slaves. They may get together and refuse to do what they are meant to be doing.

We also must remember to take as few fighting soldiers as we can away from their proper duties.

(X.20)

48. Criminals and public slaves

To Trajan
When I am in doubt, Master, you kindly allow me to write to you. Although you are our Emperor, you can lend an ear to my request without demeaning yourself.

This is my problem. In most cities here, especially Nicomedia and Nicaea, there are criminals who have been condemned to the mines, the amphitheatre and places like this. These criminals are now doing the jobs done by public slaves and they are getting paid for it.

Ever since I first heard about it, I have not known what to do. Most of the criminals are now old men. As far as I can tell, they now live honest and decent lives. I felt it would be too hard to punish them after such a long time. However, I did not think it right to go on having criminals as public employees. But I did not like feeding them at public expense either, if they did not work. But it would also be dangerous not to feed them. So I felt I must not do anything until I had written to you.

Perhaps you want to know how men who have been condemned as criminals could get out of being punished. I myself tried to find this out but I have not been able to. I have seen the sentences which were passed on them when they were in court. But I have not seen any evidence for setting them free from their punishments. Some of the criminals say that they were set free on the orders of Roman **proconsuls** and Roman **legati**. This makes sense. No-one would dare to set criminals free without the orders of someone in authority.

(X.31)

49. Trajan tells Pliny off

To Pliny
The reason why you were sent into that poor province was

because there were many things which had to be put right. I see we must remind you of that.

What you mention is exactly the sort of thing which must be put right. Criminals, who have been sentenced to be punished, have been set free and no Roman has ordered this. Even worse than this, they are also being treated as if they were honest public employees.

All those, who have been sentenced within the last ten years or who have been set free with no proper authority, must serve out their sentences. If any are too old or have been sentenced over ten years ago, let us send them to do those jobs which are most like prison jobs. They can look after the public baths. They can clean out the drains. They can repair the main roads and streets.

(X.32)

50. Pliny wants a fire brigade

To the Emperor Trajan
I was away visiting a remote part of the province when a great fire broke out at Nicomedia. It destroyed many private houses and two public buildings, even though a road ran between them. There were three reasons why the fire spread so far. First of all, a strong wind helped it to get going. Secondly, when it had got going, no-one did anything much about it. I understand that people just stood about and watched, without lifting a finger to help in the disaster. Thirdly, it spread so far because the town does not have a fire engine, a fire bucket or any fire-fighting equipment. I have already given orders and these will be bought.

Would you, Master, please decide whether I ought to set up a fire brigade. I think 150 men will be quite enough. I would make sure that only firemen were chosen. I would also see to it that they only did what firemen are allowed to do. I do not think it will be difficult to keep an eye on 150 men.

(X.33)

51. Trajan says no

Trajan to Pliny

I suppose you think that because other places have fire
brigades it will be all right for Nicomedia to have one. I think
not. There is one thing you must remember. Bithynia is a
different province and those cities have been troubled before
with organisations of that sort.

People find all sorts of reasons for getting together. When
they have got together, they call themselves all sorts of names.
You and I know that they soon turn themselves into trouble-
makers. It is quite enough to provide fire-fighting equipment
and tell the owners of the houses how to use it themselves.
They can also call on any spectators for help.

(X.34)

52. Problems in building a theatre, baths and a gym

To Trajan

The people of Nicaea, Master, want a theatre. They have built
most of it but they have not yet finished it off. It has cost
more than 10 million sesterces, so I hear. I have not yet
shaken out the accounts. But all the money has been wasted.
The theatre is sinking into the ground. It has huge cracks
which have started to gape open. This is because the soil is
damp and soft, and the stone from which it is built is loose
and crumbling.

Should the theatre be finished, left as it is or pulled down?
When you see the supports and foundations, they look as if
they cost a lot of money. But they will not hold it up. Also
many rich citizens have promised to add other things to the
theatre. One has promised to pay for a colonnade around it.
Another has promised to build a gallery on top of the audi-
torium. But they cannot make a start on this until the building is finished off.

These same citizens of Nicaea want to rebuild a gymnasium.
This was burnt down before I came. They now want to make
it much bigger than before and they have already spent a lot
of money on it. I think the money has been wasted because it
is spread over too wide an area and the buildings do not fit
together properly.

There is another point. I have met an architect here. He is a rival to the architect who was in charge of the work at the gymnasium. He thinks the walls are not strong enough to hold what is going to be built on top, even though they are 22 feet thick. This is because the walls are made of rubble and not lined with brick.

The citizens of Claudiopolis are making a set of baths. You could not call it 'building' because they are digging them out from a great natural hollow which is overlooked by a mountain. They are going to pay for them from the money which the rich citizens pay when they become town councillors. You will remember that you are the one who kindly chooses them to be councillors.

Here then are two problems. The citizens of Nicaea are not spending public money properly. The citizens of Claudiopolis are doing something very different. You have given them a gift which money cannot buy. They are taking advantage of you. This is far worse than not spending money properly.

I must ask you to send an architect who can look at both the theatre and the baths. He must decide whether it is worth finishing off the walls now that they have been started and money has been spent on them, or if it would be more useful to put right what has to be changed and move what has to be moved.

We must be careful. When we try to save what has been spent, we must not throw away any more money.

(X.39)

53. Trajan tells Pliny to make up his own mind

To Pliny
You are on the spot and must consider, as best you can, what to do with the theatre. Let me know what you decide. When the theatre is finished out of public funds, get the other citizens to build the other parts with their own money. They should do this because they have promised to do so.

Those silly little Greeks cannot keep away from gyms. The citizens of Nicaea clearly bit off more than they could chew. They must make do with what will do for them.

You must decide what to say to the citizens of Claudiopolis

about their baths. It is quite clear they have started to build this in the wrong place.

There are architects around you. Every one of our provinces has men who know about building and who can use their brains to overcome problems. Don't think it is quicker to send one from the city to you. We usually get ours from Greece anyway!

(X.40)

54. How to save money

To Trajan the Emperor
Master, I have been looking through the accounts of the city of Byzantium and seeing how much money they spend. I find they spend a lot of money. Every year they send a special ambassador all the way from Byzantium to Rome, to offer you their loyal greetings. This costs 12,000 sesterces. I know how you feel about spending public money like this. My own view is this. They should not send a special ambassador but just send the letter of loyal greetings. If they do this, they will both save money and do their duty to you.

They also spend another 3,000 sesterces every year to send another ambassador off with more loyal greetings to your governor in Moesia. I think this must be cut down in the future.

Master, I ask you to write back and tell me what you think. Please think it worth your while to approve what I have done or correct me where I have gone wrong.

(X.43)

55. Save it!

Trajan to Pliny
My dear Pliny, you have done the right thing. There is no need for the citizens of Byzantium to spend 12,000 sesterces on sending an ambassador to Rome with loyal greetings. You were quite right to ask them not to do it. They will do their duty to me if they send the letter through the **Imperial Post**.

My governor of Moesia will also forgive them if they pay a little less attention to him.

(X.44)

56. Dishonesty, corpses and treason

To Trajan, the Emperor

I have been recently working from the governor's residence at Prusa. I was coming to the end of my official business there and was about to leave when a local magistrate came to see me. He told me that a Claudius Eumolpus wanted to see me on some official business. This is what had happened.

There had been a meeting of the local City Council. At this meeting Cocceianus Dion wanted the city of Prusa to take off his hands some building work which he had been responsible for. Eumolpus said that Dion should present his accounts to the city before the work was handed over. He felt that Dion had been on the fiddle.

He also said that a statue of you had been set up in a place where Dion had buried his wife and son. He insisted that I should hold an official enquiry.

I said that I would hold an enquiry straight away. But Eumolpus said he wanted more time to prepare his case. He also asked if I could hold the enquiry in another city. I replied, 'I will hold the enquiry at Nicaea.'

When at last I sat down at Nicaea to hear the case, Eumolpus wanted to put it off again. He said he was not yet ready. At the same time, Dion, the man he was accusing, wanted the enquiry to begin. They had a great argument. Some of what they said had nothing to do with the case. Other things they said did have something to do with it.

In the end I thought I must delay the case and ask your advice. This is an important case which will be seen as an example to others. I asked both of them to put down in writing what they had to say. I wanted you to be able to see what they themselves said and make up your own mind.

Dion said he would put down in writing what he had to say. Eumolpus said he would only put down what he wanted to ask on behalf of the City Council. He was not going to mention the statue and the corpses. He was only standing in for Flavius Archippus who had told him what to say. This Archippus was with him and said he would also put in writing what he had to say. I have now waited many days but Eumolpus and Archippus have not given me anything in writing. Dion has sent the letter I enclose.

I have seen your statue in the library with my own eyes.
They say that Dion's wife and son are buried in the forecourt
of the library.

I ask you, Master, to stoop to direct me since this is a legal
matter. Many people here want to know what will happen.
This is what you can expect when the facts are known and
each side defends itself by quoting examples from elsewhere.

(X.81)

57. Forget about the treason

Trajan to Pliny
My dear Pliny, you do not need to be at all anxious about
asking my advice on this matter. You know very well how I
feel about this. I do not want to frighten people into respect-
ing me. I do not want to make people respect me by putting
them on trial for treason. So forget about the trial for treason.
I would not allow it even if other Emperors have allowed it in
the past.

'Shake out' the accounts which show the work that has
been done under the care of Dion. The city of Prusa must
know this. Dion may not refuse nor should he refuse to give
this information.

(X.82)

58. Happy birthday

To Trajan the Emperor
I pray that you will enjoy this birthday and very many others.
I hope that all men in time will praise your glory and goodness.
Safe and brave as you are, I hope that you will out do your
own great deeds.

(X.88)

59. Thank you

Trajan to Pliny
I thank you for your good wishes and prayers for me, my dear

Pliny. I want to have many more, most happy birthdays in our land which is now so lovely.

(X.89)

60. Mumbo-jumbo

To Trajan, the Emperor

If I have anything I am not sure about, Master, I always write to you. You set me right when I am off course. You correct me when I am in the wrong.

I have never been present when Christians have been put on trial. So I do not know how they are usually punished. I am also not sure what efforts I have to make to go out and find them. Here are some questions which have given me great difficulty.

1. Does it make any difference how old they are? Or should you treat children and adults in the same way?
2. Do you let them off if they repent? Or is it 'Once a Christian always a Christian'?
3. If they have committed no other crime, should they be punished for just being called a 'Christian'? Or should they be punished for the crimes that often go along with the name of 'Christian'?

This is what I have done with those who were named to me as Christians. I had them brought in and asked them face-to-face if they were Christians. If they said 'Yes', I asked them a second time. If they still said 'Yes', I asked them a third time. And this time I threatened them with punishment. If they still said 'Yes', I ordered them to be beheaded. Whatever it was that they said 'Yes' to, they must be punished for being so obstinate and stubborn. I was quite clear about that.

There were others who were just as lunatic. Because they were Roman citizens I have made an official note of it. They must be sent to the city.

But you know how it happens. When you start to deal with anything, it becomes very complicated. People here are now making all sorts of different accusations. Someone has put out a little book but he has not put his name on it. In this book are many names. There are some people who say that they are not Christians. They also say they have never been Christians. When I get these in court they repeat after me Roman prayers to Roman gods and to your statue. I have your statue brought in with the statues of the gods. They then burn incense and offer wine to the gods. And last of all, they curse Christ. This is something which real Christians cannot be made to do. If they do all this, I let them go.

There are others who say they were once Christian. They also say they are not now. Some stopped being Christian two years ago, others before that. There are some who stopped twenty years ago. Everyone of those has worshipped your statue and the statues of our Roman gods. They have also cursed Christ. If they are to be blamed for doing wrong, they only did the following things. They used to meet together before dawn on certain days and sing a hymn which had parts to it. In that hymn, they honoured Christ as a god. They also swore an oath. This was not to make them stick to each other, when they were committing crimes, not at all. They swore *not* to do these things: to steal, rob, or commit adultery; to break any promises; to refuse to pay back money to the man who lent it them, when he wanted it back.

When they had done this, the meeting broke up and they went away. Later they came together again to take food — the food itself was ordinary stuff and would not harm anyone. I told them to stop this and they have. I was following your instructions here. You have asked us to be careful over political meetings. I also tortured two slave girls who were called 'deacons of the Church' to find out what was true. This is all I have been able to find. Christianity is a lunatic and exaggerated load of mumbo-jumbo.

I have put off any more trials and I have run to you for help. I must have your advice because there are so many people who are at risk. They are people of all ages, of every class in society, both men and women. The infection of that disease has broken out in the cities. Worse, it has also spread into the villages and into the countryside. But it can still be stopped and corrected. This is already happening. People are now beginning to fill up our temples again. Before, no-one used to go. They are now holding religious services which they had once given up. In the past you could not buy an animal to sacrifice. Now you can buy them everywhere. You

74

can easily see how men can be corrected if they are allowed to repent.

(X.96)

61. What to do about the Christians

Trajan to Pliny

You did the right thing, my Secundus, in 'shaking out' the cases of those who were named to you as Christians. There is no one rule which will cover everything. The matter is so complex. But the Christians must not be hunted out. If they are named and proved Christians, they must be punished. If someone says he is not a Christian and shows it by praying to our Roman gods, then grant him a pardon. He has repented and that will do. Do this even to those who may be suspected of having been Christians in the past. Do not take any notice of lists of names that have no significance. They must not be used as evidence in a court of law. That sort of thing is a very poor example to others. It is not the sort of thing I want to be remembered for as Emperor.

(X.97)

62. Parties, money and bribes

To Trajan the Emperor

When people here come of age, get married, become a magistrate or dedicate a public building, they like to have a celebration. They usually invite all the City Council and also quite a lot of other people. They also give out one or two **denarii** as presents.

I ask you, please write and say what they ought to celebrate and how far it should go. This is what I think. We must allow them the right to invite people, when they have something proper to celebrate. But this does not make sense when they invite a 1,000 or more. They seem to be offering people bribes.

(X.116)

63. You are right

To Pliny
You are quite right to be afraid of what is going on. When people are invited like this, it looks as if they are being given bribes. This is true where so many are invited and come in groups to receive presents. They do not come as if invited to a private ceremony.

I choose you to be an example to all. By your wisdom you must direct how people are to behave in that province. By doing this you will bring lasting peace to the province.

(X.117)

64. Pliny is unsure about helping his wife

To Trajan the Emperor
Up to this time, Master, I have let no-one else use the Imperial Post. I myself have used it only on Imperial business. But I have been forced now to use it for a personal reason.

My wife recently heard of the death of her grandfather and wanted to be with her aunt. I thought it would be hard to say that she could not use the Post. If you are going to comfort someone in their sorrow, you need to get them quickly. As you can see, my wife did this for family reasons. I knew you would approve of this.

You have been so kind to me in the past. I felt it would be wrong of me to keep from you yet another example of your kindness to me. I know, had I consulted you, you would have said, 'yes'. But if I had consulted you, it would have been too late.

(X.120)

65. Trajan says it is all right

Trajan to Pliny
You are quite right, my dearest Secundus. You know how I would feel about this. Even if you had waited to consult me, my answer would still have been the same. Your wife has a duty to increase the comfort she can give her aunt by arriving quickly.

(X.121)

Epilogue

We do not know where or when Pliny died. It is likely that he did not come home to Comum but died out in Bithynia. This last letter is about a person who dies away from home. Something like this might have been written about Pliny.

66. Dying away from home

To Pompeius Saturninus

Your letter moved me in many different ways. Some parts made me happy, other parts made me sad. I am happy that you are being kept in the city. I know you do not want to stay there but I want you to. You say that you will give us a reading as soon as I arrive. I thank you for waiting for me.

I am sad that Iulius Valens is seriously ill. But I suppose it isn't sad when it would be better for him to be set free from the disease that no-one can cure.

I am sad too that Iulius Avitus has died when he was on the way back from the province where he had been quaestor. He died on a ship, far away from the brother who thought the world of him, far away from his mother, far from his sister. All this does not matter much to him now he is dead but it did while he was dying. And it still does to those who live after him. Here we have a young man snuffed out in the very spring of his youth. If only his great qualities could have matured, he would have won the highest political honours. How he burned with a love for literature! Think of what he had read! Think of what he had written! All that has now vanished and none of his descendants will reap any benefit from it.

Why do I go on like this? Once you start, you cannot stop. I shall put an end to this letter and an end to the tears which the letter has forced out of me.

(V.21)

Appendix · Another account of the eruption of Vesuvius

This is an account written by Xiphilinus, who produced a shortened version of a history of Rome by Dio. Dio wrote his history at the end of the second century A.D.

Enormous men, in great numbers, suddenly appeared. They were much bigger in size than ordinary men and they looked just like the giants in the paintings. They were seen sometimes on the mountain, at other times in the country and cities around it, wandering over the land day and night, and flitting through the sky. And after this came terrible droughts and sudden devastating earthquakes. All the flat land in the area boiled up and the tops of the mountains jumped into the air. There were echoes that came from below the ground and that sounded like thunder. Other echoes came off the earth and sounded like animals bellowing. The sea joined in the great noise and the heavens re-echoed it. Suddenly after this a horrific crash was heard. It sounded as if the very mountains were crashing together. And first of all enormous blocks of stones were thrown into the air, as high as the mountain tops themselves. After that there was a great fire and smoke that never seemed to stop. The whole sky was turned to black and the sun was completely covered up, like an eclipse. So there was night at daytime and darkness when it was light.

Some people thought that the giants were rising up in revolt again. They claimed to have seen the shapes of giants through the smoke, and what is more, some had heard the cry of trumpets. Others believed that the whole universe was collapsing into chaos or fire. And so they ran away, some from the houses into the streets, others from inside outside, from the sea to the land and from land to sea. They were so confused that they thought anywhere was safer than where they were at the moment. All this went on at the same time.

Ash was also blown up from the mountain (you could not

begin to say how much of this there was) and it covered the sea, land and sky. The ash did serious damage to men, places and cattle. It destroyed all the fish and birds and what is more, it buried two whole cities, Herculaneum and Pompeii. At the time the people were sitting in their seats at the theatre at Pompeii. So great was the dust that it reached Africa, Syria and Egypt. It also reached Rome where it filled the sky and darkened the sun. For many days those who did not know what had happened or could not guess went about in a constant fear. They all thought that everything was being turned completely upside down, that the sun was disappearing into the earth and that the earth was going up to the heavens. At that time the ash did not do any great harm to the people of Rome but later it cast upon them a terrible plague.

Glossary

Atrium. A large, ornamental hall.

Centumviral Court. The court in Rome that dealt with wills and inheritances.

Concubinae. Harems kept by some wealthy Romans.

Comoedus. An entertainer.

Consul. One of the two most important Senators; they presided over the Senate.

Consular. A person who had already been a Consul; a man of Consular rank.

Consul-elect. Someone who had been chosen to be the next Consul.

Council. The Emperor had his own inner Council of advisers; this was not the same as the Senate but there would have been Senators in it.

Denarii. Roman coins worth four sesterces.

Duumviri. Mayors.

Familia. Household; this includes family, slaves, freedmen and close friends.

Freedman. A slave who has been given his freedom.

Haruspex. A fortune teller or soothsayer.

Imperial Post. Special transport, kept for officials, and special messengers of the Emperor.

Knight. The Knights were wealthy men and almost as important as Senators.

Legatus. Governor of a province that the Emperor looked after.

Military tribune. A junior officer in the Roman Army.

Peregrinus. An alien; someone who was not a Roman citizen.

Praetor. A political office; a stepping-stone to becoming Consul.

Princeps. Another word for the Emperor (it means 'the first person in the land'); the Emperor was also known as Caesar.

Procurator. An official who collected the taxes for the

Emperor in his provinces; normally a Knight and not a Senator.

Proconsuls. Governors of provinces that the Senate looked after. All Proconsuls served as Consuls first.

Quaestor. Someone who helped the governor of a province collect the taxes.

Reading. When an author had written something he would often invite his friends round to hear him read it.

Saturnalia. A celebration usually held on December 17th when masters and slaves changed places for a day.

Senate. The Council which helped the Emperor govern Rome and the Roman empire.

Senator. A member of the Senate. Senators came from the leading families. They were the richest and most powerful men after the Emperor. Senators could become Consuls, Proconsuls and generals and hold other important positions. Senators were often away from Rome commanding armies and governing provinces.

Sesterces. Roman coins; the main unit of Roman money. It is impossible to say exactly what one was worth in today's money. We do know that a Roman soldier was paid 1,200 in a year. To be a Knight a Roman needed to have 400,000 sesterces.

Tablets. Notebooks made of small, flat pieces of wood covered in wax. You wrote in the wax with a sharp point. The 'pages' were held together with string.

Tribune of the people. A junior official or magistrate in Rome.

Index of important names and
main themes

Note: only the most important places are listed here. All the places Pliny mentions are marked on the maps. The numbers refer to the letters. The big letters, e.g. E, refer to the introductions to the chapters.

Trajan. 17, E. (Emperor from A.D. 98–117)

Tacitus, Cornelius. 2, 18. (Roman historian and orator)

Vienna. 28. (Town in France south of Lugdunum; Vienne)

women. 3, 4, 5, 6, 7, 8, 11, 17, 19, 20, 30, 36, 56, 60, 64, 65.

writing. 1, 2, 4, 5, 22, 29, 31, 32, 33, 36, 37, 38, 40.